COME TO THE FATHER

AIDAN NICHOLS, OP

Come to the Father

An invitation to share the faith of the Catholic Church

ST PAULS

ACKNOWLEDGEMENTS

The author and publisher are grateful for the following permissions to reprint:

Catholic Herald Ltd, for an earlier version of material used in the Introduction and Conclusion in *The Catholic Herald* for 23 July 1999.

The Liturgical Press, for an earlier version of material used in Chapter 3 ('The Fleshtaking') in *Epiphany. A Theological Introduction to Catholicism* (Collegeville 1996), pp. 88-9, 92-4.

A. P. Watt Ltd., on behalf of The Royal Literary Fund, for permission to quote G. K. Chesterton's 'O God of Earth and Altar'.

The English Province of the Society of Jesus for permission to quote G. M. Hopkins' 'Pied Beauty' and from his 'As Kingfishers Catch Fire'.

The Trustees of the Estate of Hilaire Belloc for permission to quote his 'Ballade to our Lady of Czestochowa' and from Sonnet VII.

The Centre for Policy Studies, for permission to quote from David Selbourne's *Moral Evasion*.

While every effort has been made to contact the copyright holders of extracts used in this book, this has not always been successful. Full acknowledgement will gladly be made in future editions.

Cover image: Masaccio, *The Baptism of the Neophytes,* Florence, Brancacci Chapel (c.1424–c.1428).

ST PAULS Publishing
187 Battersea Bridge Road
London SW11 3AS, UK

Copyright © ST PAULS 2000

ISBN 085439 603 9

Set by TuKan DTP, Fareham, UK
Printed by Biddles Ltd., Guildford, UK

ST PAULS is an activity of the priests and brothers
of the Society of St Paul who proclaim the Gospel
through the media of social communication

*My Love has been crucified; in me there is no spark of
desire for mundane things, but
only a murmur of living water that whispers within me,
Come to the Father.*

Ignatius of Antioch,
The Letter to the Romans

CONTENTS

Preface   9

Introduction   11

  1.   Faith in Truth   21

  2.   Fathering the Creation   36

  3.   The Fleshtaking   48

  4.   The Rose in the Crown   61

  5.   Ultimate Sacrifice   71

  6.   Gracious Spirit   83

  7.   Our Mother the Church   90

  8.   Holy Persons, Holy Gifts   107

  9.   Antidote to Evil   127

 10.   Homecoming   142

Conclusion   147

Sources for citations   153

Preface

When Annabel Robson of ST PAULS Publishing read a piece of mine on 'The Conversion of England' in the *Catholic Herald*, she offered me a challenge. Could I write a book about Catholicism that might actually induce at any rate one man or woman (preferably English, but not necessarily so!) to embrace the faith? If I were right about the incomparable truth, goodness and beauty of revelation, it should surely not betoo difficult to make it seem inviting. As a priest-theologian, and Dominican friar, I found it hard to refuse. For both the prophetic office of the priesthood and the missionary charism of the Order of Preachers commit one to evangelise, while the 'theologian' part puts the emphasis on evangelising not only hearts but also, and especially, minds. I had already written a rather lengthy 'Theological Introduction to Catholicism', following a thematic order chosen by myself, and published in America, under the title *Epiphany. A Theological Introduction to Catholicism* (Collegeville, Minn.: Liturgical Press, 1996).* In this book I have had the opportunity to do something briefer, following the order of the Apostles' Creed – the 'Old Roman Creed' as the scholars call it. This has required me to concentrate on essentials, not, however, with a view simply to presenting what C. S. Lewis called 'mere Christianity' (venerable as that is), but rather to open the reader's eyes to how these essentials are seen by Catholicism. The extracts of poetry at the start and in the course of each chapter have the same aim. The articles of this short Creed, summarised in the chapter titles, were once the charter of a Christian civilisation in England and the starting-point, in these islands, for all coherent understanding of the world. If the Church is to revivify, in new converts as well as in her members of long standing, this can only be through the redeployment of the energies, imaginative and intellectual, which the Creed represents. For the 'inexorable decline' to which a number of commentators have consigned English Catholicism to be reversed, for Christendom to re-awaken here, and souls to find their way to the Father from out of waterless wastes and surrogates for the truth, there is nowhere else we can begin.

I would like to thank my English Dominican confrères Denis Geraghty and John Patrick Kenrick for their helpful comments on the manuscript.

Blackfriars, Cambridge
Feast of St Augustine of Canterbury, 2000

---

* The reader who wishes to explore further about the Catholic faith is advised to make his or her next port of call *The Catechism of the Catholic Church* (Revised edition with corrections, London: Cassell, 1997). The present author has written a two-part commentary on the *Catechism: The Splendour of Doctrine. The 'Catechism of the Catholic Church' on Christian Believing* (Edinburgh: T. & T. Clark, 1995; *The Service of Glory. The 'Catechism of the Catholic Church' on Worship, Ethics, Spirituality* (Edinburgh: T. & T. Clark, 1997), which may be helpful in seeing the wood for the trees.

Introduction

O God of earth and altar,
Bow down and hear our cry.
Our earthly rulers falter
Our people drift and die;
The walls of gold entomb us,
The swords of scorn divide,
Take not thy thunder from us,
But take away our pride.

From all that terror teaches,
From lies of tongue and pen,
From all the easy speeches
That comfort cruel men,
From sale and profanation
Of honour and the sword,
From sleep and from damnation,
Deliver us, good Lord.

Tie in a living tether
The prince and priest and thrall,
Bind all our lives together,
Smite us and save us all;
In ire and exultation
Aflame with faith and free,
Lift up a living nation,
A single sword to thee.

The need for religion

A human being without a religion is unnatural, as is
a society that finds itself in the same boat. There is
in people a deep-rooted instinct to put the largest questions

11

to the universe even if – like you and me, dear reader – all they know of the world be aspects and fragments. Indeed, it is a desire to locate the meaning of the elusive whole that drives them. And as soon as they realise that the whole must be marvellous, they begin to worship, to practise rites that conjure with the name or names of the divine. The saddest of all atheists is the person who puts the question of the meaning of everything but then suppresses his or her desire to marvel because they know of no direction in which to kneel. Religion is as natural – as intimately congruent with our nature – as any other of the main activities in which, since the appearance of man on earth, we have passed our time.

The need for religion does not stop there. Religion is not only among our most basic drives, so that we should expect to find it practised in the most primitive of places. It is also among our highest propulsions, so that we can expect to encounter it in the most civilised of scenarios. A human being without a religion cannot be fully civilised, any more than can an agnostic society. Without a pervasive perception of a transcendental truth, goodness and beauty conferring coherence and abiding value on human life and action, no high culture can be lastingly sustained. A 'secular' society lives off the capital – intellectual, moral, artistic – of the religious past.

Take England today. How could a society be called either natural or civilised if sport and politics, shopping and sex (that oddly assorted foursome) were its only enthusiasms? These are all sectorial occupations, very well – on certain conditions – in their place. But within what scheme of living are they to take their bearings and find that place? How can each be saved from its excesses (or, for that matter, from the cynical repugnance excess always brings)? How can even good things be saved from skewing, spoiling? Only by re-casting within some wider scheme where the motto is, A place for everything and everything in its place. And that holistic picture only a great religion can provide. In Britain today the secular culture often makes people feel that 'social permission' for religion has been withdrawn. This is one of our culture's most depressing – and oppressive – features. And even those people who escape the taboo sufficiently to say, 'I'm not religious *but...*' may get no further than a few New Ageist delvings (a spot of geomancy, a touch of spiritualism, some parings from the Indian or Far Eastern religions, along with a light powdering of residual Christianity) which scarcely fits the bill if a coherent vision of the whole is what is wanted.

Or look at the matter from another angle. The quartet of activities I have mentioned are inherently competitive – shopping less so than the rest, though there are always auctions and the January sales. A modest dose of competition sharpens our wits. But what will become of a society where people are 'joined' only by a sense of their individual rights? Is not such a joining more truly a separation? Where is the glue that will bond people together – in friendships and families, neighbourhoods and cities, nations and on earth – if secular liberalism has its way? Not least among secular commentators, the fear is that society, and so the people who compose it, is not only getting trivialised, though that is bad enough. Worse, it is becoming unstuck. A great religion renews all these bonds by furnishing fresh rationales and motives for honouring them, and leads people to treat others in these varied constituencies as precious, not as essentially invasive competitors on the playing-fields of the self.

But it must be the true religion!

No great religion is without its elements of truth. Without elements of truth, a religion would be unable to frame a credible context for human life; to instil a sense of due proportion among life's different activities; and to legitimate and motivate the ties that keep people together in the pursuit of the good. It would be unable to inspire literature or philanthropy, spirituality or art. However, such pragmatic tests, for all their symptomatic importance, cannot give the entire picture. If religion orients us to reality – and above all to that wider realm in which the world as we know it is set – then reality, so described, must be allowed *its* say as well. It is not enough for a religion to include true elements. It must as a whole correspond to the ground of things and be validated by that ground, even as by human effort it continues to seek to reflect it.

Now it is of course rather unlikely – to put it mildly – that any purely human construct could by good luck or good management do any such thing. That is why Plato, in commending his own philosophical purification of ancient Greek religion, proposed it as only provisionally the best account going. His proviso is that, if a word about human affairs should reach us from God himself, then even the best available human construct would need to be adjusted accordingly. Reality is always speaking to us: not only in other people but in the fruits of our labours in the vegetable garden, the response to our efforts with a sluggish car engine, or the stone on which, in a celebrated proof of its independent being, Dr Johnson, in kicking it, stubbed his toe. Could not transcendent reality – the ground of the world –'speak' in yet another of the analogous ways in which the real communicates? As the example of Plato shows, it is no part of the work of philosophical reason to exclude such a possibility. It will be reason's task to assess it, and the chief way it will do so is by evaluating how much further transcendent reality's 'speaking' (we call it *revelation*) allows us to see. What sort of new perspective does it open up? The test of the true religion is that it leaves in our hands a truth than which no greater can be conceived, a truth that can integrate all other truths (including the elements of truth in the other religions) within a pattern that is supremely satisfying aesthetically and morally, supremely fulfilling of the human desire for beauty and for goodness. But the *essence* of the true religion is that it can be credited on the very word of God himself, who since he *is* truth, can neither deceive nor be deceived. By it (in the words of the prophet Isaiah [51:1]), we return to the rock from which we were hewn. We come to the ground of all that is. We come – as we shall see – *to the Father*.

The objection may be posed that the present author would predictably say as much being born as he was in what in 1948 was arguably a Christian country, and certainly into a believing if not practising Christian family. How otherwise could he be in possession of a christening certificate from a diocese of the Church of England showing him at the age of less than two months to have been made 'a child of God, a member of Christ, and an inheritor of the kingdom of heaven'? And if, in since becoming a Catholic (as distinct from Anglican) Christian he has shown a degree of elasticity of temper, this is hardly of a nature to suggest extreme intellectual adventurousness! All such arguments hit the nail on the side. No one can speak except from some specific location, out of some particular kind of education, and from within some tradition of human experience. If that universal fact is to be taken as subverting the claims of every speaker then no truth – not even of engineering science or English grammar – can be generally upheld. But as a matter of fact, outside of lunatic asylums or post-modernist university faculties, we do not treat the cultural particularity of people as ruling out the general truth of their assertions. We do not regard someone's origin as the criterion for the validity or otherwise of their utterances. We consider what comes out of them, not from what place they come. The only respect in which *my* origins are pertinent to the account of Catholic Christianity in this book is the one mentioned in the Preface: as the poetic citations which open each chapter suggest, the book is offered especially to my countrymen and countrywomen, the English – within (perhaps I had better add to pre-empt accusations of Little Englandism) the framework of the

15

British, with their relations with Europe and beyond, within the unity of the human race at large.

Meanwhile allow me to enter again the plea, addressed in the first instance to fellow believers, which was the occasion of the commissioning of this book.

Converting England

Both the last General Council of the Church – the Second Vatican (1962–1965) – and the post-Conciliar popes have encouraged Catholic Christians to try to read the 'signs of the times'. I believe one vital sign for the renaissance of Catholicism in England is to be found in the new debate over English identity – itself largely catalysed by events North of the Border. If it can be shown that Catholic Christianity was not only essential to the making of England (an historical claim) but also provides the best foundation – intellectual, moral, social, aesthetic – for the remaking of England in the future (a philosophical or theological claim along the lines of my remarks earlier in this Introduction), this will greatly help others to get clear the scope and shape of the faith and to gauge its true worth. This offers a strategy for the mobilisation of believers, for encouraging them to enter a debate about the wellsprings, the roots, the chief historical determinants of the English contribution to civilisation which is also a debate about the future orientation of an English culture and society, steadied, hopefully, by a firmer grasp of its historic patrimony.

The 'politically correct' refusal to speak about the conversion of England for fear of offending ecumenical or inter-faith sensibilities as well as arousing humanist–secularist irritation is based on an unfortunate misreading of the documents of the Second Vatican Council. Those documents certainly mandated courtesy, respect and the seeking of common ground in dialogue with such different constituencies as separated Christians, adherents of other world religions, humanists. But they do not understand

16

such dialogue as entailing the cessation of mission, or as putting into cold storage the universalist claims of the Catholic Church. As the Council's 'Decree' on the Church's missionary activity, *Ad Gentes*, puts it: according to the divine plan

> the whole human race is to form one people of God, coalesce into the one body of Christ, and be built up into one temple of the Holy Spirit. (7)

And a little later the same text adds:

> It is not enough for the Christian people to be present and organised in a given nation. Nor is it enough for them to carry out an apostolate of good example. They are organised and present for the purpose of announcing Christ to their fellow citizens by word and deed, and of aiding them toward the full reception of Christ. (15)

But how well fitted is the Catholic Church in England – the so-called 'English Catholic Church' – to launch a new mission to the people of England, remobilising energies ecclesial and sacramental and so ultimately gracious and salvific, in the context of the question, The Church once made England, can she now remake this not terribly impressive culture of supermarkets and sport? In point of fact, and despite the gloom-and-doom merchants, I think the Church here *is* quite well equipped to take up this mighty challenge, and the reason is that it is not the 'English Catholic Church' – a Church of ethnically pure men and women, operating as an independent barony – at all. Rather is it a Church that is something of a 'dog's dinner' or, to put it more complimentarily, a *pot-pourri*, which includes, yes, recusant families and converts from Anglicanism or their descendants but also a large constituency of Irish people and those descended from *them*, as well as Italians, Poles and other southern and eastern Europeans, incomers from the New Commonwealth, Filipinos and a host of others. Now if the original (Anglo-Saxon) conversion of England is anything to go by, what you need for a successful movement of conversion – one that really 'takes' and acts to transform culture across a whole society – is precisely a mixture of indigenous and exogamous elements: people from inside and people from outside. The great figures of the development of Christianity in Anglo-Saxon England included, certainly, Cuthbert and Wilfrid, who were of pure English stock, but also Augustine the Italian, Theodore of Tarsus the Greek, and Aidan who was a *Scotus* or (more or less) what we would now call an Irishman. And really it stands to reason. If the protagonists of mission come exclusively from *within* the culture, it will be difficult to see with sufficient objective distance to judge what its baptism requires. If on the other hand they come exclusively from *outside* the culture, they will lack the inner sympathy for it, and that ease of identification with its members which are pre-requisite for winning people. If one could imagine the journalist Mary Kenny, say, and the abbot of Downside rolled into one, *there* would be the perfect apostle for the conversion of the English!

English identity is in flux, and there are many thoughtful folk who find the consequent bewilderment disturbing. They have only to look to the Venerable Bede's *History of the English Church and People* to see how things stand. English nationhood was born in the waters of the baptismal covenant, in the setting of the mission of the universal Church. The novelist E. M. Forster had abandoned Christianity, but when he soliloquised in the narrator's voice about the identity of England he dropped his guard.

> The water crept over the mud flats towards the gorse and the blackened heather. Branksea Island lost its immense foreshores, and became a sombre episode of trees. Frome was forced inward toward Dorchester, Stour against Wimborne, Avon towards Salisbury, and over the immense displacement the sun presided, leading it to triumph ere he sank to

rest. England was alive, throbbing through all her estuaries, crying for joy through the mouths of all her gulls, and the north wind, with contrary motion, blew stronger against the rising seas.

What did it mean? For what end are her fair complexities, her changes of soil, her sinuous coasts? Does she belong to those who have moulded her and made her feared by other lands, or to those who have added nothing to her power, but have somehow seen her, seen the whole island at once, lying as a jewel in a silver sea, sailing as a ship of souls, with all the brave world's fleet accompanying her towards eternity?

So the 'identity of England question' can provide the Church with a providential re-entry into a public discussion which interests a wide range of people and touches all. At the same time the fact that, in our high culture, the intellectual style increasingly prevalent, if also increasingly controverted, is that of post-modernism, makes it very desirable that something like this *kind* of answer to the question, Why are we here? be forthcoming. Post-modernism is a sort of philosophy whose central thrust it is to make the fragmentary the ultimate. It denies that any story – 'meta-narrative' they call it – can in broad outline tell it all. It abandons hope for any truth that can be a sky under which all can shelter, there to live and love, play and rest secure.

Our culture and its discourse appear to be splintering into broken shards; interest groups and single-issue lobbies have at best one or another of the severed pieces. There is, too, a general disquiet about a sense of moral decline that seems to be more than simply the sour grapes of the old at the wild oats of the young. It is all very well for politicians and pundits to set moral aims for society. Such aims will never be effectively pursued where they stand alone as objects of the social will. They require the support of the metaphysical certainty which dogma guards, and the inducement, imaginative and emotional, of the ceremonious habits of a community acquainted with prayer. Liberal democracy depends on pre-modern moral capital, and presumes qualities in human life that require virtues that are cultivable only in environments of a definite kind.

In this situation the need will eventually be felt for an architectonic schema, a vision where everything falls into place. Will other churches contribute to this? Of course, and I have indicated in some of my other writings how I see that – notably in regard to the 'repatriation' of Eastern Orthodox doctrinal and spiritual themes (*Light from the East. Authors and Themes in Orthodox Theology* [London: Sheed and Ward, 1995], *passim*), and the strong compatibility with Catholic thought of elements of historic Anglicanism (*The Panther and the Hind. A Theological History of Anglicanism* [Edinburgh: T. & T. Clark, 1992], 'Conclusion'), and the manner in which these Christians could be *united* with the Catholic Church but not *absorbed* (*Christendom Awake. On Re-energizing the Church in Culture* [Edinburgh T. & T. Clark, 1999], chapter XIII). But this is coming home to the House of Peter, where all apostles and disciples belong. And that much-needed 'architectonic schema' which these contributions (and others) could fill out, is precisely what 'Catholicism' means. It is thinking, acting, praying, living that goes *kat' holon*, 'by the whole' – recognising the human thirst to be in touch with totality. When that need is acknowledged, that need for a great home in which all can dwell, the Catholics of England can point to the house of Anselm and Newman, of Mother Julian and Sir Thomas More, and say, Here, in England, there is accessible to you the very house of God and the gate of heaven. It will be the aim of this book to show how that can be.

Faith in Truth

'I believe…'

Firmly I believe and truly
God is Three, and God is One;
And I next acknowledge duly
Manhood taken by the Son.
And I trust and hope most fully
In that Manhood crucified;
And each thought and deed unruly
Do to death, as he has died.
Simply to his grace and wholly
Light and life, and strength belong,
And I love, supremely, solely,
him the holy, him the strong.
And I hold in veneration,
For the love of him alone
Holy Church, as his creation,
And her teachings, as his own.

Rational preamble

SINCE this is not a study of Christian philosophy – though
the Catholic faith has brought into being a considerable
body of philosophical thought – I can here be brief. No
one whose mind has not become cluttered or clouded by
the wrong sort of reading is likely to question the *penchant*
of the mind for knowing the real. In the rational preamble
of faith we remind ourselves of what unstudied reaction
implicitly takes for granted, that our minds are so suited to
reality that there is really no limit to their capacity for it,

and their desire for it. Reality comes in various shapes and sizes, of course, and some may find the varieties of dahlia more absorbing, others the battleships of World War II. One can 'go off' certain people, but it is unusual to find someone who has lost all interest in human persons at large – even if, as with sadists, the interest involved is inseparable from perverted and perhaps diabolic energies. This boundless quality to our knowing and our desire to know is a symptom of the single most important fact about us, our being made with an inbuilt tendency towards God, a natural desire for him.

Two arguments for the very existence of God have by implication already been touched on. The perfect fit between our minds and the world they know – a matching so fruitful that all technology springs from it – strongly suggests that the origin of the world lies in an infinitely creative Analogue of the finite intelligence which is ours on earth. The tendency of the human mind to reach out beyond its native heath, delighted by the manifold forms of being in the world around it, and to exhaust the world before it is itself exhausted, definitely points to its intended destiny in a union with a reality so altogether boundless that nothing greater can be conceived. So God is the world's origin, and our goal.

Catholic philosophy makes use of quite a panoply of arguments to indicate, in, through, and beyond experience how, like light refracting in a rainbow of colours, all substances with their diverse values issue from one transcendent Source, and how, too, all perception of them and the language in which our evaluations are expressed make covert appeal to the truth and perfection of that ever-flowing Wellspring of whatever is. And the upshot? All truth, beauty, goodness, pre-exists in that single Fountain of being, which is fullness overflowing. All that is in the world around us exists and acts by participation in that Source. All the perfections we know in creatures co-exist in utter simplicity in that changeless Light.

The idea of revelation

In a largely secular society, the very idea of thinking and acting that is *dependent on revelation* easily becomes inaccessible. In the contemporary Church as found in the countries of the North Atlantic civilisation, the historic homelands of secularism, the notion of revelation often eludes the grasp of Christians themselves, unless a serious doctrinal effort is made to affirm and explore it.

Revelation has two presuppositions that are altogether basic. First, the world around us is endowed with a capacity to be 'iconic': to image or echo its divine Creator. That ability of the created order – whether as a whole or under some aspect or in some particular instance – to point to its divine source is the basis for 'natural revelation', the disclosure of God in created being that underlies the world religions in different ways, as well as in myth and literature, dream motifs and art. Over and above this, it belongs to the Creator to be able to enhance the iconic potential of things in such a fashion as to serve a saving design for the repair and consummation of the creation – to act as vehicles for the 'second gift' of salvation which is to make good and *more than make good, take beyond itself*, the 'first gift' of created being itself.

But then second, man – the human animal – must be able to interpret aright the revelatory force of things (no 'disclosure' can be successful until it finds its recipient). In the case of humanity after the Fall, with our darkened and error-prone (though still truth-directed) intellect and our distorted and weak (though still goodness-seeking) will, that interpretative work needs the help of divine grace even with regard to natural revelation. But with supernatural revelation, it follows from the nature of the case – from the kind of divine activity involved – that the human person could not scan aright its epiphanies in the experience of prophets and apostles, nor grasp correctly the lessons those epiphanies contain, unless our natural human powers of knowing and willing, thinking and loving, were super-naturally energised, were raised up into a new order of activity that corresponds to the purpose of God in his saving self-disclosure.

What makes revelation possible from the side of God? Here also there are two principal presuppositions we must mention. First, as the philosophy of religion can tell us – at least when providentially steadied in its intellectual gaze and thus sharpened in its argumentative focus – there must be in God a communicative freedom analogous to, though infinitely exceeding, that ability to disclose our purposes and so the direction of our personalities which charac-terises the (microscopic) spiritual beings we ourselves are. As the creative Archetype of those gifts God must enjoy a liberty in self-communication of which our experience, as creatures that live by language and friendship, is only the dimmest reflection. But secondly – and here only the biblical proclamation, as found in the Church's apostolic rule of faith, can serve our turn – revelation from the side of God is only possible if in fact God *desires* us as his conversation-partners, desires, indeed, to share his life with us. It is the faith of the Church that the God who is from all eternity a living Act of self-communication (Father to Son in the Holy Spirit) has elected to share with human beings the knowledge and love he has of himself in his own triune life, with a view to not only healing our corruption but bringing us to Glory.

Revelation is, then, a wonderful conspiracy of created potential with the divine will. 'By light, light', said the Jewish sage Philo of Alexandria, and the disclosure of the one who is 'Light from Light' as Jesus Christ intensifies that illumination. The light of revelation is, we can say, not only a 'Thaboric' light, shining on our senses through epiphanies in the incarnate order (the paradigm here is the radiance of the face and raiments of Christ as he was transfigured on a mountain – 'Thabor' – in the sight of his disciples). It is also an intellectual light that shines from within (our Creator is more intimately present to us than we to ourselves), enlightening our understanding, inflaming our will.

Our current difficulty in grasping what 'revelation' may be derives from the institutionalised intellectual pride of the post-Renaissance Western cultural tradition. Much of the intellectual and cultural leadership of early modern and modern Europe set out to close the minds of those they influenced to penetration by the light of revelation, a light whose transcendence requires, uncomfortably, the intellect's submission. That sin of intellectual pride taken with full seriousness by the spiritual masters (it is a plausible explanation of the Fall of the angels) – became embodied in educational and civil institutions, and pervasively 'around', finally, in the mental air we breathe. It has been, in the twentieth century, a major part of the vocation of Christian poets so to discipline our sense for the effulgence of creation – the lesser light – that our intellectual eye may be re-sensitivised to the epiphanies of supernatural revelation – the 'Greater Light' as the chorus calls it in T. S. Eliot's *The Rock*.

> O Light invisible, we praise Thee!
> Too bright for mortal vision.
> O Greater Light, we praise Thee for the less;
> The eastern light our spires touch at morning;
> The light that slants upon our western doors
> at evening,
> The twilight over stagnant pools at batflight,
> Moon light and star light, owl and moth light,
> Glow-worm glowlight on a grassblade
> O Light invisible, we worship Thee!

Revelation's realisation in its midpoint, Jesus Christ

Eliot's range of examples of the lesser light of creation reminds us that, indefinitely 'open' as the powers of our soul may be, we are none the less earthlings – for whom the light of day and its extinction at night are crucial to our biorhythm, who need the roof, walls and domesticity of homesteads, and share an environment with other species. It was, accordingly, altogether appropriate that the supreme epiphany to serve as revelation's vehicle took the form of the Word's Incarnation, when he who is as the Great Creed (the composite Creed of Nicaea–Constantinople, produced in two stages, 325 and 381) proclaims 'Light from Light' was seen as a babe at his human mother's breast. The Incarnation, celebrated liturgically in the Church of the Byzantine rite under the superlatively fitting title of the *Theophany* – the epiphany of God in his own person – unfolds its purpose in the subsequent events of Jesus' childhood, Baptism, public ministry, and – above all – in his suffering, death and Resurrection and their aftermath, the coming of his Pentecostal Spirit, the Spirit of divine–human fullness. For it is here that we see the *scope* of revelation in its full measure. Here, in the Christ of the Nativity and the ensuing scenes of the incarnate life up to the Cross, the rising from the tomb and that mystery of presence in absence which is Pentecost, we see both revelation's amplitude and its goal.

As the definitive revelation both of the divine and of the human, and therefore of their inter-relationship, and in the new light he throws by his words and action on the earlier history of revelation in the 'Elder Covenant' with Israel and on the created order itself, the incarnate Word makes available to the world the greatest truth the world has ever known or can know. This is the 'greatest' truth because it possesses more far-reaching implications than any other, and because it is more wonderful, more inexhaustibly than any other the appropriate object of that admiration or wonder which Aristotle identified as philosophy's true point of departure. Here is revealed what St Thomas Aquinas called so simply *iter ad Deum*, the 'way to God'. 'I will give you as a light to the nations,

that my salvation may reach to the ends of the earth'
(Is 49:6).

From revelation to Tradition

From revelation to Tradition is no great step, since Tradition
in the high theological meaning of the word, dignified by
an initial capital letter, *is* revelation as registered by the
corporate mind of the apostolic Church. The revelation in
Christ, which is also revelation *as* Christ, would not have
been a *successful* supreme disclosure of the way and will
of the triune God in his saving outreach to us unless it was
suitably received into the minds of its first and most crucial
destinees, the apostolic founders of the Church. The
question of whether the media of revelation in its
transmission are to be thought of as only written (the
position of the sixteenth-century Protestant reformers) or
as both oral and written (as Catholicism and Orthodoxy
hold) is really a subsidiary one, though much ink – and
even blood! – has been spilt over it. The main thing to get
hold of is Tradition's essence: Tradition is the aboriginal
inhering of revelation in the corporate consciousness of
the apostolic witnesses. That is why the best modern
Catholic theology treats Sacred Scripture as a monument
of Tradition – the chief monument of the great Paradosis –
and not as an alternative to Tradition. To say that something
belongs to Tradition in the high theological sense – to
Holy Tradition – is not as yet to make any comment on its
written or non-written form.

It is because Holy Tradition inheres in the Church's
'deep' – that is, not always explicitly conscious – mind as
the Church built on Peter and the Eleven, that the *primary*
virtues she must practise in its regard are fidelity and good
stewardship, not theological creativity and pastoral
ingenuity (these come later).

The gift of revelation to the Church constitutes Tradition.
That word ('tradition') to which the modern stream of

27

consciousness spontaneously attaches such epithets as 'cramped' and 'hidebound' denotes, rather, the unbounded generosity of the true and living God. I wrote there the *living* God, thinking of how the salvation which is revelation's content is not only what God has done and does for her but also what he has been and is for her. The revelatory gift includes its Giver – the triune Lord in Jesus Christ. That is why the Church has always possessed Tradition's plenitude. But I also wrote of the *true* God, because the life of the Church in springing from his self-disclosure, though it be a hidden and mysterious life is not for all that an 'illogical' or 'undogmatic' one. Far from it! The Church very definitely has a *logos*, a message to communicate, a doctrine to teach. The Son of God did not come to the Church as Word without truths to convey, nor did the Spirit of truth come to her as Paraclete, to complement the mission of the Word, without bringing to the apostolic mind all that Jesus had taught the Twelve, and leading them into 'all the truth' (Jn 16:13). Thanks to the twofold economy of the divine Word whose cutting power is sharper than a double-edged sword (Heb 4:12) and the divine Spirit, subtle in his wisdom (Wis 7:22), Tradition, though it be the comprehensive vision which fills the Church's mind, is also doctrinal substance. Faith is not some vague 'vision thing', strong on uplift but weak on truth-claims. It involves acts of apprehension, conception, recognition, as we assent responsibly to the truth that inheres in God's self-revelation to mankind. In the corporate faith of the apostolic community, Tradition is delivered to *understanding* hearts.

Now among the truths with which Tradition tingles, those concerning the God-man are going to be crucial. Just as revelation's midpoint is Jesus Christ, in the acts which embodied in a series of wonderful 'epiphanies' his unique being and consciousness as the God-man, so Tradition's centre is the apostolic witness to the meaning of his atoning work and saving teaching.

The Mass as the milieu of Tradition

The Church entertains the Tradition in the milieu of the Mass. That is where, *par excellence*, the Church reads the Old and New Testaments in the unity of the canon of Scripture (all sixty-six books of it!) as the biblical Word addressed first and foremost to herself, the Spouse of Christ, in the here and now of the assembly of her faithful. As the homilies of the patristic period, the age of the Fathers, and their continuators in later times indicate, she finds in those Scriptures the narrative of the triune God's self-revelation – with its climax in Christ the Head and its consequences in the life of his body the Church. Here the key is the 'typological' reading of the Bible where events in the far distant past throw light on the centre-point of salvation in Christ, and that central event of all history throws light forward in its turn to the time of the Church in which we ourselves live, to illuminate our spiritual effort and our ultimate goal. That kind of interpretation of the Bible is already suggested by its inner structure, and it is positively mandated by the ancient liturgies of Christian East and Christian West alike. Look, for instance, at the stained glass windows of King's College, Cambridge, or of Chartres.

But it is not only the fore-Mass, the Mass of the Catechumens, the liturgy of the Word, that is Tradition's milieu, the setting where the apostolic registering of revelation is at its most palpable. In the Eucharistic oblation itself, the Church, by the power of the Spirit, re-actualises the mystery of the Lord's saving work on the Cross, in the Murial, and at the Easter tomb. In the Eucharistic Prayer – the 'canon' not this time of Scripture but of the *Mass*, the Church does not – she cannot – separate the remembering of her Saviour, his identity and work, from the daily rediscovery of who she herself is as the Bride made immaculate on the Cross and so the mediatrix of his Sacrifice. (The section of the Mass liturgy called the *anamnesis*, the 'Remembering', makes that plain.)

So all doctrinal understanding in the Church is linked to the liturgical 're-actualisation' of Scripture and to the celebration of the mysteries of Christ's life which are also – by the Lord's gift – her own. To find out what the Catholic Church makes of revelation, it should be enough, then, at least in the first place, to come to Sunday Mass where a significant *soupçon* is available.

Scripture as Tradition's primary monument

Catholics are not 'bibliolaters' yet their Church has endless veneration and love for the Scriptures: Tradition's most signal expression. Of course the Gospel was 'traditioned' before any apostle or amanuensis or follower of an apostle ever set pen to parchment. Revelation – and so Tradition – is bigger than any expression of it, even one so capacious as Scripture. And yet, when we reflect on how in the modern period, with the rise of that subjectivism typical of the nineteenth and twentieth centuries, the idea of religious *truth* readily evaporates to be replaced by the warm steam of religious *psychology*, it becomes clear how necessary it was for revelation to enter, through Tradition, object form – the kind of plain, unmistakable object which it takes no effort for a book to be. The hard outlines of this book – the Bible – safeguards an ecclesial subjectivity that really is authentic, authoritative, because it was apostolically received. Boosting Scripture does not mean, as some Protestants seem to think, taking the Church down a peg or two. Quite the contrary. It is to protect the Church's sense of faith from being expropriated by groups or individuals with their self-set agendas that Catholicism looks to Scripture, rejoicing in its sharp, clear difference from all human projection.

So Tradition – revelation in transmission – becomes text as Holy Scripture. Thanks to the charism – the gift – of *inspiration* received by the hagiographs – the sacred authors, and the consequence of that charism, which is *inerrancy* in all that concerns (even factually, in matters of history or natural science where pertinent) saving truth, and thanks also, when the canon of Scripture is constructed, to the locating of the limits of the literature that bears these hallmarks (inspiration, inerrancy), the Church can point to this body of texts in all its glorious objectivity. And so she does, both negatively, by way of admonishing those Christians who prefer to do their own thing, not God's thing, and positively, in helping people to grasp what it is she has, by revelation, in her mind. The Church gazes into the mirror of the Scriptures, and she sees there not so much her own face as her own *faith* as the Bride of the divine Word.

Tradition's other media of expression

However, as the Catholic episcopate, gathered together under the dark sky of the Protestant revolt, were painfully aware at the Council of Trent, Scripture by itself cannot suffice to render the full Gospel proclaimed by the Church's preaching, celebrated in her sacraments, lived out in her ethos. Either because not all of articulable Tradition has passed into the biblical text or because the full meaning of that text is not recoverable by scanning of its content alone, the Church cannot rely on the Bible only. If the content of Tradition were not to suffer a diminution that truncated the Gospel, the Tridentine Fathers reasoned, that Tradition must be recognised as enjoying twofold form. There are not just the Holy Scriptures. There are also the divinely originated oral traditions necessary to complement or elucidate the Bible's full meaning. The crisis over the sources of revelation was resolved by the Council's insistence on parity of esteem, with Scripture, for traditions about faith and morals continuously maintained in the Church because coming 'from the mouth of Christ' or otherwise 'inspired by the Holy Spirit'.

But where are these divinely originated oral traditions

to be found? In a host of other monuments to which Catholics look to find the revelation of God in Jesus Christ his personal Word. These can be verbal, as with the baptismal Creeds – augmentations of those summaries of the apostolic preaching we find in the Book of the Acts of the Apostles. Verbal likewise are the texts of the Church Fathers who play a role in the transmission of Tradition second only to the apostles themselves. In the way the Fathers registered the Tradition that had found its objective medium in Scripture – in the way they received the biblical revelation – they acted, under God, as makers of the Christian religion in its final form, summarising and clarifying the rule of faith, establishing the grand lines of the historic liturgies and, not least, determining that crucial canon of Scripture.

The 'score' of the Church's liturgies is also of course in part verbal, made up of language, but with the liturgy – considered not now as the milieu of Tradition in the (upper case) singular but as a monument of the traditions in the (lower case) plural, we also broach the *visual* medium, for the liturgy is enacted in gestures and supremely in the sacramental signs. Visual too is the witness to Tradition of the Church's art, where, at their most evangelically ambitious, iconographers attempt a rendering of the whole Gospel in visual form, an artistic counterpart of the written Gospels and indeed of the message of the Bible as a whole, coming to a head as this does in the New Testament proclamation. As Catholic Christianity understands things, divine revelation is not only audial but visual, not only verbal but ocular – which is why iconography is so outstanding a witness to Tradition, to the fullness of the revealed truth proposed in Scripture. The inseparable character of these media – the preached words of the Word and the sensible signs of his actions – is also attested in the lives of the saints, formed as they were by the apostolic preaching to be, in the pattern of their lives, its visual expression. The saints are revelation's living seals.

There is also such a thing in the Church as unwritten traditions – in matters, especially, of worship and discipline – *originating from the apostles themselves* as men endowed with a unique authority to determine what divine revelation had left open in the life of the Church as a believing, worshipping, acting and praying people. One thinks here, for instance, of the putting in place of the orders of bishop, presbyter (priest) and deacon as the local 'applications' of the apostolic office, and the way that, at the council of Jerusalem, the apostles set aside the need for circumcision and the rest of the ritual Torah (the Jewish Law) as conditions for the entry of Gentiles into the covenant life of the Church. One could add: the establishing of the main Hours of Christian prayer (later to be the divine Office), such liturgical gestures as the Sign of the Cross, and doubtless much in the concrete form of the sacraments, as well as the continence or abstinence from marital relations of bishops, if not priests. What is common to the contents of such a list is being *apostolically given* – but this, evidently, is not the same thing as oral tradition divinely originated which was, rather, *apostolically received*. The 'apostolic tradition', then, consists of Tradition plus the traditions the apostles left behind. Sorry about the complication which, though, usefully alerts us to the fact that wealth (and here are tremendous religious riches) always means complexity. This is as true of the Church's inheritance as it is of personal property. It is not hard to guess whose life is simpler, Paul Getty II or a Carthusian hermit.

The need for a magisterium

It might be thought that the Catholic's good fortune in being able to contextualise Scripture in so profusely flowering a garden of theological delights – everything from Caravaggio to the Armenian liturgy – would make it easy to interpret Scripture, Tradition's objective correlate.

But steady on! First of all richness is all very well, but there is such a thing as an *embarras de richesse* as well. Christians unsympathetic to biblicism as excessively narrow and to theological liberalism as dispiritingly thin are often attracted, as with High Anglicans, to the kind of 'multimedia' portrait of Tradition I have been painting. But if at the same time, as with such Anglicans, they are hostile to, or lack the experience of, a sacred teaching office, they soon find that, faced with the bewildering variety of Tradition's monuments from numerous points in space and time, they are as much launched on a sea of private judgement as any primitive Lutheran or, for that matter, sophisticated Latitudinarian. In the Church's ecumenical Councils and the *ex cathedra* judgements of her popes the Creeds are extended by reference to further aspects or entailments of themselves, just as the same Creeds came into existence as expansions of the brief dogmatic nuclei in the New Testament itself (such as the affirmation, 'Jesus is Lord' (1 Cor 12:3). Episcopate and papacy – assisted, evidently, by theologians who are (or jolly well should be) learned in the lore of Tradition's multi-faceted expression, interpret these multifarious monuments by virtue of the 'charism of truth' the apostolic ministry exercises in fulfilment of the promise of its Lord. In this way we become aware of 'new' – to us – doctrines: fresh articulations of the tacit content of the 'given' of Tradition, the precious 'deposit' of faith. For the most part, such dogmas are dramatic examples of doctrine hard won, honed in intellectual strife. But all the time, every day, in the ordinary preaching of the Church's pastors (the Pope for the universal Church, the bishop for the local church), the same process is continuing, more gently and therefore less remarkably – unless, that is, what is taught enters into sharp collision with the *Zeitgeist*, something we see happening where the Catholic teaching on sexuality (always within marriage, always at once unitive and procreative in its meaning) is concerned.

Please notice too how the usefulness of the magisterium to 'faith in truth' is a matter of helping us to hear not just *what* Tradition has to say (the content of doctrine), but *how* Tradition says it (doctrine's overall shape or proportions). Someone may be aware of all the Christian truths discretely in such fashion that either they entertain them atomistically or exaggerate the import of one or another doctrine, thus distorting the face of revelation as a whole. For, as with faces, to change one feature is to change everything. From the sixteenth century onwards, the magisterium has accepted the task of overseeing the presentation of Christian truth through commissioning, promulgating or at least authorising and confirming *catechisms*. And that task is a vital one. We need to see the shape of our faith in its entirety, or else we shall not see the wood for the trees. So seeing is not to solve an intellectual puzzle, but to move forward on that journey of transfiguration of mind and heart and all our powers which we call growth in holiness. We cannot profit by the gifts of God unless we are taught which they are and how they are related as well as how obtained. We must be equipped for the journey to Glory.

2

Fathering the Creation

'...in God the Father almighty,
Creator of heaven and earth...'

Glory be to God for dappled things –
For skies of couple-colour as a brinded cow;
For rose-moles all in stipple upon trout that swim;
Fresh-firecoal chestnut-falls; finches' wings;
Landscape plotted and pieced – fold,
fallow and plough;
And all trades, their gear and tackle and trim.
All things counter, original, spare, strange;
Whatever is fickle, freckled (who knows how?)
With swift, slow; sweet, sour; adazzle, dim;
he fathers-forth whose beauty is past change:
Praise him.

The revelation of the Father

THAT God is our Father is the manifest claim of the New
Testament, but to scan this claim successfully we need the
interpretative assistance of Tradition to see what suchlike
words might mean. The influential Liberal Protestant
theologian and historian Adolf von Harnack, for instance,
wanted to restrict the 'essence of Christianity' to acknowledgement of the unique value of everyone, conceived in
the framework of belief in, precisely, the Fatherhood of
God. Harnack's hostility to the Church's dogma made him
miss the fact that the New Testament revelation of God as
Father is neither simply nor even primarily the attribution
of certain qualities to the divine nature. It is not only – or

even mainly – a statement about the provident care of One who knows every sparrow that falls to the ground and considers human beings of more worth than any sparrow – though, to be sure, the Gospels include such affirmations (Mt 10:29,31). Yet those qualities of the truly caring parent who is ever-attentive to the welfare of his/her children had already been ascribed, in Israel's tradition, to the God of the patriarchs, who was also the God of Moses and David, and so united in himself all the covenant relationships which bound the chosen people to their Lord through these human mediators. Indeed, in the canticle recited by the dying Moses in the Book of Deuteronomy, Israel's Lord is explicitly named as 'father' of his people, with an emphasis on both divine authority and divine long-sufferingness.

> Do you thus repay the LORD,
> O foolish and senseless people?:
> Is not he your father, who created you,
> who made you and established you? (32:6)

Of course, the New Testament confirms the Old, and nothing of the Judaic doctrine of God – his transcendence of, yet presence in, his creation, and notably his freely willed involvement with his chosen people – is alien to the teaching of Jesus and the faith of the apostolic Church. But the New Testament is far from *merely* confirming, in matters of the doctrine of God, its Old Testament inheritance.

During his ministry, Jesus had already alluded to his peculiar relation of intimacy with God, and taught that the divine claim on Israel was embodied in him. He had also spoken of the power of the Spirit of God in his words and actions. But at the first Easter, his disciples – a company of Jews (and Jewesses) who, through their sharing in the faith of Israel, possessed a true grasp of the divine reality – were suddenly confronted with a super-abundance of fresh meaning. In the events of his suffering, death and Resurrection, Jesus did not simply vindicate the claims he

37

had made about the divine nature and his place in the working out of the divine plan. More than this, there took place in those events a new disclosure of the divine, world-redemptive in force. In the bestowal on the risen Jesus of a real – tested and proven – lordship over nature and history (see the empty tomb and the transfigured One in the Garden and the Upper Room!), God reveals Jesus to be the divine Son – and by the same token reveals *himself* to be quintessentially the divine Father. And this he does by the illuminating power of the Holy Spirit now sent on the disciples from the Father through the Son – the Spirit who at the same time brings the disciples of Jesus, restored and forgiven, into a share in the love-life of Father and Son by what the New Testament calls their 'adoption' as sons (and daughters). Now we are not dealing here simply with redemptive action by a God who is, on the basis of the Old Testament, already known, but with a redemptive revelation which has as its issue the life-transforming impact of the supreme truth that the saving God is the Holy Trinity. And what this means in the first place is that God is primordially the Father. He is the Father far more fundamentally than he is the Creator, for he generated the only-begotten Son before all worlds. And, as we shall see, this changes the way in which we think about creation.

When the champions of the First Ecumenical Council, Nicaea I (325), were victorious in their struggle for recognition as authentic witnesses to the deep mind of the Church, they did more than secure the triumph of that orthodox understanding of Christ which alone makes full sense of the New Testament records. Certainly, they did that. Since God was in Christ reconciling the world to himself (2 Cor 5:19), Jesus is not, in his ultimate personal identity, a creature as we are, for of no creature could it be said that its actions were those of God himself. But more than this, the triumph of the Nicene Symbol (the Creed confessing the Son to be 'consubstantial' with the Father) vindicated faith in God as the *essentially fruitful One* – the Father –

he whose loving generativity expressed in the eternal procession of the Uncreated Son gives us the key to appreciating the basic relation of God to the world.

If the world is not a necessary work of God; if, as Scripture indeed presents it, the world is not the unfolding of the divine being (this would be some form of pantheism) but a work as freely made as that of any artist, then we *might* be justified in thinking of creation as, so to speak, thrown off by God gratuitously – taking 'gratuitously' there to be synonymous with 'atypically' or even 'carelessly'. Perhaps, if the world be, as it is, God's free creation (no transcendent Source such as was described at the outset of the last chapter could be said to be *indigent*, to *need* anything), he may regard it as something of an experiment. Possibly he may see the experiment, so far as man is concerned, as rather a failure, on which the files will in due course be declared closed. But the Creed's authoritative interpretation of the New Testament – God did not create his Son, as he created the world, but, as Father, generated him from all eternity – proves the divine nature to be something which no philosophy of religion or natural metaphysic could show it to be. Here, you see, we are moving in the realm of the supra-rational mysteries of faith, which, however, are pregnant with rationally exploitable meaning for our natural understanding. The Creed proves the divine nature to be *essentially self-manifesting fruitfulness* – in which perspective we cannot speak of God as simply 'happening to' create the world, as though this could be fortuitous and uncharacteristic, since delighting to bring into being what is not himself, so as to rejoice in its otherness, is *the* property which befits the Father's constitution as the first Trinitarian Person. It is the defining property of the Father that, himself ungenerated and so the primal Source of all that is, he none the less generates the eternal Son – and in so doing himself provides the framework of interpretation for his making of the world in time.

Everything we have to say, then, about God as our

Creator must be governed by the more primordial truth that he is Father of the Son. It is only in the Son, Jesus Christ, that the Father has revealed who he is in his own essential nature. Only because God is inherently productive is he the Creator at all. Those foolish people who maintain that 'all that stuff about the Trinity' is 'irrelevant' (to the world, understood) could hardly have got it more wrong! It is because the Father brings forth the Son from within his own being – and not, as with the world, creates him from out of nothing – that the Son, as revelation of the Father, enables us to see the world and humanity within it in a new light: as the typical result of the essential fruitfulness of God, a richly diverse and multifaceted example of that otherness issuing from himself which God loves to love. Belief in the divinity of the Son is a necessary condition for finding credible the proposition that God cares passionately for the world, rather than regards it with a distant and possibly revocable benevolence.

Not that we should forget here the Holy Spirit – about whom there will be more to say in chapter 6. The Spirit relates the world to the Father through the Son made man, for it is his role in the Trinity to place himself at the service of – nay, to *be*, the Son's fruitfulness. It is the Spirit who enables the creation to come to that completeness God wills for it – a *perfect* completeness (we call it 'eschatological', from the Greek word for the ultimate) for it is the consummation of the Father's plan. St Basil calls the Spirit the 'perfecting cause' of all creation.

You could have learned of the communion of the Spirit with the Father and the Son from the initial act of creation... The Father, since he creates by his very will, would not have needed the Son, but he wants to create through the Son. The Son would not have needed cooperation, since he acts in the same way as the Father, but he wanted to perfect the work through the Spirit... You understand, therefore, that there are Three; the Lord who orders, the Word who creates, the Breath who confirms. Who else could have been the confirmation if not the One who perfects?

Composing the creation

Viewing the creation, then, in the light of the eternal generation of the Word, and the consummate fruitfulness of that act which is the Holy Spirit, we can agree with the poet Gerard Manley Hopkins, as cited at the opening of this chapter, that God 'fathers' the world 'forth'. But what does the world, the cosmos, the composed creation, consist in?

– a pattern of interlocking physical forms, creatively imagined by God and willed by him as an ecological harmony – not without its moments of internal dissonance – which expresses at the level of creation the divine Glory, but in a mode of deficiency inevitable in what is finite. By its nature, the act of creation is unobservable since it sets up all the conditions, even logical ones, in which any observation might take place. Still, the affirmation of the Book of Genesis that in the beginning God said, 'Let there be light' (1:3) is remarkably congruent with what modern science has to say about the eruption of an ocean of fire (the 'Big Bang') from which the space–time universe burst forth. Indeed, secular-minded critics of the Big Bang once opposed the idea of an initial singularity (a uniquely dense primordial atom), exploding in a burst of cosmic fireworks, as too suspiciously biblical to be true! All organised matter is reconfigured light, as exploding stars scatter life-generating elements in space. The Genesis creation accounts betray a rudimentary cosmology, conveyed in a literary poetic that may remind us, charmingly, of the mediaeval bestiaries which, indeed, it inspired.

From the touch of the divine Word all the life-forms spring into being, leaf and fin, feather and fur, spruce and orderly – even heraldically so – and yet a-quiver with life. But this well conveys, albeit in imagistic fashion, the radical dependence of all things on the Creator God. The world had an explosive birth, but its configuration (whether by evolution alone, or other means) shows a delicacy appropriate to the act of creation which is nothing other than the prodigal but gracious gift of existence by the sole necessary Being. And what *of* evolution? The principle of inter-specific continuity is plausible and has been a major stimulus to scientific research. Yet the absence of transitional forms between genera, families, orders, classes and the phyla indicates that Darwin's notion of an evolutionary mechanism (chance mutations interacting with environmental pressure) is hardly the whole story.

– the angels, sheer intelligences, incomparably high powered, that complete the ladder of being which otherwise would reach only the hybrid (part spiritual, part physical) being of man. Scripture speaks of the graced or 'good' angels as constantly worshipping God by a heavenly liturgy, while simultaneously carrying out missions in the service of God in our universe's space–time. In the life, death and Resurrection of Jesus Christ the Bible reports a concentration of angelic presences – understandably, since the Incarnation is the throwing wide of a door between the heavenly and earthly worlds. But thereafter the angelic realm has a new centre in the Word made flesh. In her own liturgy, the Church speaks of angel guardians, who play the role of helper in individual human biographies. It may be that experiences at the limits of normal human powers (those of artistic genius, say, or scientific and mathe-matical imagination at highest pitch) are angelically assisted. The same is true for such borderline negative

42

experiences as those of extreme 'superhuman' evil. According to revelation, those angels who preferred to regard their own enormous intellectual power as self-serving rather than placing it at God's disposal now act as forces of disintegration in the world, inhibiting where possible God's saving design to raise man to share his Glory in Christ.

– the human person, situated on the boundary of the invisible and the visible, partaking of both through the intimate unity of body and soul with the latter's fine point, the spirit. The poet Hopkins wrote of the human body, '[it] deals out that being indoors each one dwells' – an attempt to render, in suggestively compressed language, how the body both reveals our innermost thoughts and feelings and yet at the same time enshrines them, encloses them. For Scripture, God created man 'in his own image' (Gen 1:27), possessing a similitude of the divine being in a more sublime way than the rest of creation, for what the body discloses is a person endowed with spiritual powers of understanding and love. The dignity of human persons is rooted in this act of being, deeper grounded than any empirical characteristic Tom, Dick or Harriet may show. And yet this exalted dignity is made manifest in various perfections, such as the freedom whereby we are the masters of our own acts, the responsibility which flows from this, the benevolence whereby we can love other creatures for their own sake, and, not least, the ability to direct all our actions toward God, our last end. Man is not just a puzzle (though the Fall makes him that), he is a mystery. But the mystery is not hard to see for it declares itself every day in those we meet, and in ourselves. As the philosophical analysis of reflective consciousness indicates, the human soul is non-material, at home in the world in the manner of a delighted explorer there (rather than after the fashion of another of the world's contents, of what is explored). Created directly by God, then, and infused into the physical matrix of life, the functioning of the brain is the necessary condition for its activities here on earth. By the same token, that is no reason to rule out immortality hereafter. Nothing is in the intellect that was not first in the lowly, earth-bound senses – save the spiritual act of understanding itself. It is because of the spirituality dwelling in flesh that Catholicism honours man as the masterwork of creation and the means to its unity in God.

St Francis of Sales wrote:

> Man is the perfection of the universe,
> the spirit perfects man.
> Love perfects the spirit
> and charity perfects love.
> That is why loving God
> is the aim, the perfection
> and the excellence of the universe.

If there is intelligent life beyond our planet and galaxy the *first* part of that statement would need modification, but not the rest. The bodies of distant thinking creatures may differ from our own, though their free intelligent life will bear *some* relation to terrestrial animality. But however different their modes of contact with revelation we could soon tell whether they knew the supernatural life or not by their awareness (or otherwise) of charity.

In scanning the cosmos, we are dealing with created participations, hierarchically ordered, in the 'Names' – the substantial attributes – of God. The True, the Good, the Beautiful, the One, being itself: these eternal lamps illuminate all thinking about the world, for they flood with light the world itself. It is the wonder of the Church's metaphysics of creation that it combines the austere monotheism of Israel – there must be no confusion between created and Uncreated, world and God, with that sense of

44

the inter-communion of all levels of reality typical of Platonism and its kindred philosophies. That is because its metaphysics have learnt from revelation the courtesy and non-competitiveness of God who by his own causal power grants to things (and persons) a natural share in his attributes, just as by grace and gratuitous affection he will grant persons a supernatural share in his inner life.

The Fall and beyond

In the Letter to the Romans (5:12) St Paul affirms the causal link which binds the present condition of man, under the dominion of sin and death, to the Adamic 'fall', that aboriginal catastrophe recorded in Genesis in a way that is archaic, certainly, yet has fascinated not only exegetes but philosophers as well. If human nature was not created with a propensity to evil – and the Fatherly inspiration of creation rules that out of court, then it acquired that propensity in history, which must mean at history's beginning since no ancient historian has yet found an actual golden age. Humanity was not born ailing. It fell sick. The Church's perception of just how sick, and how (for nature) incurably so, derives from her awareness that it took a redemptive Incarnation to put this right. St Cyril of Alexandria comments:

> Adam was created for incorruptibility and for life; in paradise he led a holy life: his mind was wholly devoted to the contemplation of God, his body was safe and peaceful, without the occurrence of any evil pleasure; the tumult of foolish propensities was non-existent within him; But when, because of sin, he fell into corruption, then pleasures and impurity penetrated his fleshly nature, the law of savagery appeared in our members. Nature became ill from sin by the disobedience of one man, that is from Adam. Thus was the multitude brought forth in sin; not that they shared in the error of Adam – they did

not yet exist – but because they shared his nature, fallen under the law of sin. Accordingly, as in Adam nature became ill from corruption, through disobedience, since the passions entered into it, so in Christ it has recovered its health; it became subject to our God and Father, and did not commit sin.

Ours is a universal, cosmic condition of estrangement from the Father, expressed in the sado-masochistic despoiling of ourselves and others, ending in a death which is fearful, the rupturing of the personal unity of body and soul.

In a world that issues from the hand of the fruitful Father it is a terrible indictment of what we have done, been and are that when we look within, we find hearts of darkness, and when we look without, we look into the living, busy world of man and see, often, no reflection of its Creator. What, then, must be done? In a fallen world, the human vocation is first and foremost to find the true face of the Father – for without a just appreciation of what sort of world this is in its provenance, its preservation and its goal, man will always be a wanderer, a lost soul, on earth. When the Church – the bearer of the knowledge of this face – is rejected by a culture, wide-ranging ill-consequences follow. In the late nineteenth century Nietzsche proclaimed the death of the divine Father in whom authority and goodness are inseparably united, the font at once of power and of value. That was, he thought, a necessary condition for the autonomy of man. Again, Freud deemed revolt against a paternal ancestor to be the origin of psychic projections of fatherly divinities that act as foci for guilt feelings typical of 'psycho-dramas' of an irrational kind. Neither Nietzsche nor Freud, the one a child of the manse, the other of the synagogue, ever encountered, we can suppose, the true doctrine of the Father as the ever-generative, fruitful, enabling divine Source, active not in competition with man but for his final flourishing. But the reaction against the Father they pioneered has produced a society and culture where fathers are instinctively distrusted;

where a spirit of unreflective parricide is abroad; where to exercise paternity, by nurture of biological children or formation of spiritual children, has become especially hard.

The collective trauma created in the Western soul by distortion of the image of the divine Father, followed by murderous revolt against him, can only be healed and pacified by return to its Catholic and evangelical source. As we shall see in chapter 5 in particular, that 'source' is the Trinity on the Cross. On Calvary it was shown to men that, while it was the Son who suffered and the Spirit by whom the Son's oblation was offered, what that oblationary suffering revealed was the Father's face – how the Father's nature, from before all time, is sacrificial through and through. Though God does not suffer there is in him the Archetype of all self-surrender and willingness, for the Beloved's sake, to endure. The Cross renews in the midst of creation that self-bestowal by the Father which was the Son's begetting before all worlds.

3

The Fleshtaking

'... and in Jesus Christ, his only Son, our Lord,
who was conceived by the Holy Ghost...'

The poet's imageries are noble ways,
Approaches to a plot, an open shrine,
Their splendours, colours, avenues, arrays,
Their courts that run with wine;

Beautiful similes, 'fair and flagrant things',
Enriched, enamouring, – raptures, metaphors
Enhancing life, are paths for pilgrim kings
Made free of golden doors.

And yet the open heavenward plot, with dew,
Ultimate poetry, enclosed, enskied,
(Albeit such ceremonies lead thereto)
Stands on the yonder side.

Plain, behind oracles, it is; and past
All symbols, simple; perfect, heavenly-wild,
The song some loaded poets reach at last –
The kings that found a Child.

The Great Assertion

THE key belief of the Church, on which everything else
turns, is the Incarnation. I call this 'the Great Assertion'
because it is of world-shaking significance that Jesus is
personally identical with the divine Son, who is himself
very God, 'Light from Light'. Clearly, the question whether
or not some human individual is thus identical with the

48

uncreated Word through whom the world was made cannot be a bagatelle. (It is, surely, the ultimate in 'gobsmackers'!) The claim that Jesus of Nazareth, not a figure of myth but someone whom historians can research, was personally united to the Godhead may be dismissed as false, but it can hardly be written off as trivial. Yet put in such terms it remains a question of theory, albeit one of vast speculative importance for our understanding both of God and of human dignity. The same question when put, as the Creeds do, in the context of salvation, becomes charged with practical import for my life and destiny. It now turns into the question, Do the deeds of Jesus Christ as found in the Gospels have only a morally inspirational value (this was another of the truly just men of history)? Or did those deeds actually change the terms of living? Did they change the terms on which the very gift of human life itself is received from God? That would be the case if in those deeds One who was personally divine was active precisely so as to re-order the origin, life-resources and final destiny of human beings, in a word to *re-make* us. He can re-make us if he acts on us in a divine, creative way, making us participate in his way of being and thus in God.

Announcing a birth

By that 'Fleshtaking', human nature was united to the Word, the second Trinitarian Person. From the Greek for 'person', *hypostasis*, we call that (and the phrase is a crucial one for Catholic orthodoxy) the *hypostatic union*. But that stupendous event entailed – as with any divine action in relation to what is not divine – the work of the entire Godhead, all three Trinitarian Persons in their undivided Unity, though without derogation from the specific role of each. The Father sends the Son; the Son allows himself to be sent, and the overshadowing Spirit fashions an ensouled body for him from the flesh of the consenting Virgin. That Virginal Conception is understood by the Church not on the analogy of spontaneous parthenogenesis in nature, as though this were a freak biological occurrence. Rather is it directly divinely enabled as a sign of the absolute novelty of the Incarnation of the Word in his own world. But is it not – like all miracles – a (literally) incredible interruption of the order of the world? To theists, the order of the world is an order of divine purpose. The miracle of the Virginal conception and birth, like the miracles Jesus will perform in his ministry, is, in this perspective, supremely orderly, not disorderly at all.

We can count the Annunciation, then, and the manifestation of what happened there at Christmas and the Epiphany, as the opening act of the Trinitarian revelation. The climax of that revelation – so important a matter that it will occupy a full chapter but we cannot omit a mention of it here – will come with the mystery of Easter, the Son's Cross, his Resurrection and the sending of the Holy Spirit. Those events are not incidental to the Incarnation. To serve its redeeming purpose they were in view from the beginning. That is why, in much Western mediaeval art, the manger of the babe of Bethlehem looks remarkably like a tomb; why in Pieter Bruegel the Elder's *The Adoration of the Kings* the infant Jesus shrinks from the proffered vessel of myrrh, symbol of his future dying; why in Giovanni Bellini's *The Madonna of the Meadow*, the slumber of this child on Mary's lap suggests not so much contentment as the sleep of death. And the Perugian artist Benedetto Bonfigli makes the whole matter plain when, in an altarpiece now in the National Gallery in London, he joins together in a single panel the Epiphany and the Cross. It is on the Cross that the Holy Trinity is climactically disclosed. The glory of God's triune love finds its supreme 'epiphany' in the human form of the Son precisely as we see his humanity broken on the Tree. 'I, when I am lifted up', with all the ironic ambivalence of that phrase (at once lifted up on the gibbet and exalted to the Father) 'will draw all people to myself' (Jn 12:32). The Resurrection, which demonstrates the victory of the Cross,

50

must likewise be a Trinitarian event: the Father awakens the Son made man from the dead so that freshly united with him he can send forth the Holy Spirit upon the Church. But none of this makes sense except via the Annunciation, when the pre-existent, uncreated Person of God the Word takes on our nature in the womb of his human mother, so as in that nature to suffer, die and rise again.

For the modern Roman liturgy, the Annunciation is more profoundly a feast of Christ than it is of his Mother – and that, despite the lovely English mediaeval name for this festival, 'Lady Day', is as it should be. The conception of Christ is an event at once biological and theological, and so is rather shocking to pagans. God entered the human race as a foetus, just like the ones we throw away daily in our hospitals. No empirical difference is observable – but *this* embryo was united personally to the Logos by whom all things were made. He became a man as we are, and so vulnerable to the worst we could do to him. The Redeemer was in the womb, that sanctuary of new life which a knife-cut can violate. But it was to be for our comfort. The Incarnation may point to the Crucifixion, our last word to the Son of God in this world. But beyond it lies the Resurrection, God's last word to us, loving his murderers to the end.

As many of the artworks of the birth of Christ in Latin Catholicism attest, the Nativity shows us in a quite literal sense the *humility of God*, for the Divinity incarnate lies on the *humus*, naked on the ground. These canvases, like the mid-winter crib scenes in and outside churches, are familiar though puzzling to the post-Christian world. Thanks to globalisation by international capitalism, this – the Christmas festival (25 December) – is one bonanza hardly anybody escapes. But how terrible for it to be a Christmas without religious memory, what the French essayist André Frossard recalled from his secular childhood: 'an amnesiac Christmas which was the feast of Nobody'. That is an increasingly common experience, because the Christmas message is getting harder to preach. In so far as this is a secular society, with a scientific – or, rather, a sub-scientific – mind-set, there is little room for metaphysics and so for a sense of the wider realm in which things are set, spaced between their divine origin and their divine goal. In so far as this is a multi-cultural society, with a variety of religions or quasi-religions jostling in the consumer market-place, there is only the feeblest understanding of the biblical revelation where ideas of creation, Incarnation and salvation belong together in a coherent way, in an account of the meaning of life, history and the world that hangs together as a whole. In the run-up to Christmas, it sometimes seems as if only those isolated bits and pieces of Christian truth which can be recycled in terms of political correctness have any future at all – like the person who said they could see no point to the Virgin birth unless it encouraged attention to the rights of single mothers!

But we are not dealing, at Christmas, with a possibly useful legend of 'Once upon a time'. We are dealing with the God who entered human history at a verifiable place and a datable time, in Bethlehem of Judah when Quirinius was governor of Syria – and that, St Paul maintained, was 'the fullness of time' (Gal 4:4), the moment when all the keys for our understanding were in place. It was after the sages of Israel had clarified for ever the absolute abyss of distance that separates the Uncreated from the created (no demigods for them), and yet drawn attention to the wondrous action whereby the Word and Breath of God hold all things in being, in a communion between the Maker and what is made. It was after, too, the providential preparation of pagan culture, through myth and ritual, for a god who is born, dies and rises again to renew the earth. It was after the prophets of Israel had set in the hearts of the Jewish people the hope for 'He who cometh' – a new visitation of God comparable not only to the Exodus, the liberation from Egypt, but to the original creation itself, and this to be bound up in some mysterious fashion with the promises to the dynasty of David. It is as much the key to ancient history as it is to subsequent time.

This central event of all history would meet us just where we need to be met. However, we analyse and categorise the disordered condition of our world, the root of the problem is evil – sin and its wages, everlasting death. In no matter what cultural epoch we live, to be saved from such is our prime necessity. The angelic voices heard by shepherds on the outer ear on Christmas night: 'To you is born this day in the city of David a Saviour who is the Christ, the Lord' (Lk 2:11) echo the words heard on the inner ear by St Joseph in his dream: 'You are to name him Jesus, for he will save his people from their sins' (Mt 1:21). Learning about this Birth is not possible without an opening to the mystical: the gestation of some events is signalised in intimations from the divine.

Accepting a mission

Among the early Christians, the name and title of the Redeemer – Jesus Christ, the Son of God, the Saviour – was rendered by an 'acrostic' drawn from the initial letters of these words in Greek: *Ichthys,* 'The Fish', something which not only provided them with a useful code name (and code drawing, or cryptogram) for their religion, but reminded them that the Lord's mission like their own salvation had *begun in water.*

In *The City of God*, St Augustine remarks that 'Ichthys' is the mystical (the hidden) name of Christ 'because he descended alive into the depths of this mortal life as into the abyss of waters'. His Baptism is a crucial moment of transition, as the perfect Israelite passes like the people of the Exodus of old through the waters where God had declared them his chosen people by signs and wonders, and also prophesies his own passage on the Cross from death to life. For St Ephrem the Syrian, it is all part of Christ's coming down, putting on Adam's nature as a garment so that Adam could put on glory. The Baptism is not only the manifestation of who Jesus is: the Son of God, endowed with the Spirit who descends on him. It is also the beginning of the glorification of our humanity. The descent of the Dove (visible symbol of the Holy Spirit) signifies both. Along with the Transfiguration – and, as we shall see, the Cruci-fixion and Resurrection – this is the great theophany of Jesus' ministry. The Father is revealed to hearing, the Son to the touch (of John the Baptist), the Spirit to sight. From then on, we know the perspective in which we are to see all Jesus' actions (and his 'passions', his sufferings) and hear his words. After Christ is revealed as the Word, a fifth-century Armenian catechism says, the Son, standing in our midst, shows the Father and the Spirit to the world.

Not only as God but also as man, the Saviour exists in his relation to the Father in the unity of the Holy Spirit. In his personal existence, as deployed in time, on the earth of our planet, he *is* the revelation of the Holy Trinity. Jesus lived by the Holy Spirit whom he received, and the vision of the Father with whom he spoke in prayer and whose bidding he did. The drama played out in the life of Jesus cannot be explained without reference to the primordial interplay of God's inner life: the mutual love of Father and Son in the Holy Spirit. It is true that the doctrine of the Trinity has only been made known to us through the Word made flesh. It is not the result of reason working on the materials of general experience. But it is equally true that we cannot properly understand Jesus Christ unless we get the hang of the threefold relationship expressed in his life and consciousness – unless, that is, we acknowledge God as the Trinity.

Communicating a message

But what did he *say*? By the end of the first year of the ministry it was clear that Jesus' message differed from that of John the Baptist in two respects. First, he placed less emphasis on the negative moment of God's judgement of Israel and more on the positive moment, soon to be realised, of her restoration. Second, he stressed the concomitant salvation of all the nations for whom Israel was meant to be a light. In his public preaching, Jesus proclaimed God as not only Judge but Saviour. He spoke of salvation as not simply the result of human decision and effort but also as the gift of God. Indeed, he spoke of the human decision for salvation and the effort to gain it as part and parcel of that very gift. The only thing he asked was that this gift of salvation be accepted as a *total* gift – in other words, in the most radical poverty of spirit (thus his 'Beatitudes', Mt 5:1-12). That went against the grain of the Jewish religious parties of his day, who preferred to rely on their own works, and notably the observance of the Old Testament Law. This aspect of his teaching, exemplified in the parable of the Pharisee and the tax collector (Lk 18:9-14), would be especially well understood by St Paul.

But what was this 'salvation' that Jesus held out to his hearers and saw his own preaching as inaugurating? He saw it as the coming of a new paradise, as is made clear by his sayings on marriage. Divorce is now prohibited, for the norm of paradise is restored, and this is possible because a cure for human hardness of heart (the problem that had led the Old Testament to allow divorce) is now to hand. Thanks to Jesus' presence and influence, the disciples are becoming changed people. The rigour of his ethical demands upon them (no hatred, no lustful thoughts) only makes sense on the understanding that human nature is being transformed, thanks to communion with him.

That this was not self-delusion was shown in the miraculous signs of salvation Jesus worked. The exorcisms he carried out were meant to point to God's imminent triumph over evil, the dawning of his reign. The miracles of healing and such miracles in nature as the calming of the storm and the multiplication of the loaves and fishes point to the restoration of physical nature, its harmonisation with what is good for human beings, and a superabundant fulfilment for the life of the old creation.

The coming about of the reign of God, at which Jesus aimed in his public teaching and action, had, then, its cosmic aspect, but its centre lay in the relations of persons to God. In his table fellowship with sinners, regarded by the Jews of the day as ritually unclean, Jesus reversed the hitherto normal biblical order by putting communion before conversion. Without acquiescing in the sins of these reprobate characters, he first of all extended fellowship to them in the Father's name, and that turned out to trigger repentance and so conversion. His extraordinary freedom displayed itself not in an abstract criticism of accepted standards, but in making himself accessible to those who needed him, regardless of conventional limitations. The meals he took with the disreputable he regarded as anticipations of the banquet between God and humanity at the end of time. That Jesus understood this offer of communion with God as including (eventually) the Gentiles is shown by the parable of the mustard seed which grows into a great shrub in which birds can nest. 'Birds' was, at the time, a common metaphor for the Gentiles; 'nesting' was a technical term for their eschatological assimilation to Israel. Because this 'programme' involved the restoration and integration of the depressed elements in society – the poor, the sick, the simple – a later age whose own outlook was sociological and humanistic rather than metaphysical and religious could misconstrue Jesus as a social reformer.

Alongside his public or 'exoteric' teaching lay a private or 'esoteric' message delivered to the disciples alone. The turning point, beyond which Jesus begins a deeper and more mysterious-sounding instruction of the disciples, is Peter's confession of Jesus' Messiahship at Caesarea Philippi (Mt 16:13-20). In his response to Peter, Jesus defines his aim as the Messianic task of building a living 'temple', as on rock, secure against decay, the temple of the last days. He was referring here to the eschatological temple which, in the Hebrew Bible, symbolised the final meeting-place of God and humankind, the site of their definitive communion. In the symbolic thinking of the period, this temple was conceived as miraculous, everlasting, the centre of a new heaven and a new earth, the goal of pilgrimage for all nations. How did Jesus understand his role in creating this permanent divine-human communication?

As the final revealer of God's will and the agent through whom that will was to be realised, the construction of this temple fell to him personally, but he could not achieve it until he had first become victorious over the anti-God powers at work in the world – sin and death – and thus been enthroned at God's right hand. At his trial, Jesus was accused of having said, 'I am able to destroy the temple of God and to build it in three days.' (Mt 26:61). Why should that particular statement have been taken as blasphemy? In an oracle from the Second Book of Samuel, God is made to say of the future Messianic king:

> He shall build a house for my name, and I will establish the throne of his kingdom forever. I will be a father to him and he shall be a son to me (2 Sam 7:13-14a).

'Forever': originally this was deliberate hyperbole, court rhetoric, but Jesus treated it literally. Unless he had referred to himself as an ever-living or eschatological Messiah, we cannot understand why his disciples, after the first Easter, took the Resurrection appearances as proof that their crucified Teacher had turned out to be the Christ of Israel, the 'once and future king'. At his trial before the Sanhedrin, the high court of Jewry, Jesus refuses to conceal his Messianic character for fear of implicitly abandoning this eschatological claim. In any case, now helpless in his enemies' hands, the title 'Messiah', 'Christ', had lost its liability to political misinterpretation: Jesus would become a suffering Messiah, a Messiah of the Cross. Yet to claim to be Messiah, albeit forever, would not itself be regarded by

57

other Jews as blasphemous. Something more was involved. The last line of the oracle suggests what it was: 'I will be his father and he shall be my son'.

Jesus understood his eschatological Messianic sonship in a sense entirely his own. He spoke of himself as 'the Son', absolutely or unconditionally, and uniquely. When speaking with the disciples he was always careful to say, 'My Father and your Father'. *'Our Father'* was what he told the disciples to say, not what he said with them. Part of his unique sonship, as Jesus understood it, was sharing in the divine prerogatives *vis-à-vis* creation. From the moment of Peter's confession onwards, we find the two themes of Jesus' Messiahship and his cosmic enthronement joined together. In these contexts he often spoke of himself in terms of the figure called 'The Son of Man', that angelic representative of suffering Israel, described in the Book of Daniel as receiving power and glory from God to triumph over the forces hostile to his people. This constellation of ideas recurs at the climactic moment of Jesus' trial.

> Again the high priest asked him, 'Are you the Christ, the Son of the Blessed One?' Jesus said, 'I am; and "you will see the Son of Man seated at the right hand of the Power", and "coming with the clouds of heaven."' Then the high priest tore his clothes and said, 'Why do we still need witnesses? You have heard his blasphemy!' (Mk 14:61-64).

It was as a Messianic pretender who also claimed to share in the divine attributes that Jesus was condemned for blasphemy.

After Peter's confession, Jesus' esoteric teaching became an initiation of his disciples into the meaning of his suffering and death. As the Messiah, whose enthronement, itself stunningly supernatural, transcendent, would not come about without his own violent death, he had the power to, as he put it, 'ransom' the mortal and the dead. The Son of Man had come to 'give his life a ransom for many' (Mk 10:45), which is a Semitic way of saying for all – not just for a remnant of Israel but for all Israel; and not just for all Israel, but for all the world. His death and subsequent enthronement would purify the world from sin, and by thus overcoming its alienation from God the Creator give it entry into a new life.

Predicting the Passion

The blank wall of incomprehension Jesus could meet even from intimate disciples (as well as later students of the Gospels) is visible from the scene (Mt 20:7-28) where James and John – and their mother, co-opted as their advocate – have come to accept Jesus' Messiahship but understand it, against the Old Testament background, in largely this-worldly terms. They seek to be his vice-gerents in a Jewish theocracy which will rule the world. But, as Jesus explains, not only is his Messiahship on another level from that of worldly power. He will enter on its exercise only with his (literally) excruciating death. Catholic teaching allows us to understand what this means. The uncreated Son of God, now existing in our human nature cannot make that humanity share in the divine Glory until his human nature and personality 'replicate' or mirror what he is in his divine reality, the only Son of the Father. And that will happen on the Cross when his sacrifice, offered for our sake in loving obedience to the Father, *perfectly represents what he is from all eternity.* As Son he is eternally turned to the Father in love by a self-giving which is divinely fruitful because from it there comes the Holy Spirit. Calvary will picture the Trinity, and more than that by conforming the created structure of our humanity to the inner movement of the Trinity, the Cross will enable our humanity to share in God's Glory. By the Cross Jesus will be lifted up as king, as Messiah, a fact revealed in the Resurrection.

So the only 'sign', the only external confirmation of the truth of his teaching he will give 'this generation' is the 'sign of Jonah – the preaching prophet who, thrown overboard by fear-maddened sailors in a storm, had spent three days in the belly of a great fish. Jesus may perform miracles out of charity or compassion. He may let people or situations extract them from him. But the only sign he absolutely wills, rather than permissively allows, is the sign of Jonah. And as the version of this saying in St Matthew's Gospel (12:39-42) makes clear, its content is the death, burial, the three days' sojourn in the tomb, and the resurrection. But why is *that* the sign *par excellence* of the truth of Jesus' message? The answer to this question will point us ahead to chapter 5 of this book, '*Ultimate sacrifice*'. In his death and burial the Lord Jesus entered a condition of which *our* death, appalling a prospect as it is, gives little indication. The unnatural parting of soul from body will be for us, in Newman's words, agony and ruin. But beyond this Jesus suffered what Scripture calls the 'second death', the experience of the world's sin: 'Hades' or 'Sheol', those biblical names for the 'place' of Godlessness. In his atoning act he who knew no sin was 'made to be sin' in St Paul's graphic phrase (2 Cor 5:21). With all those sharpened spiritual powers which belonged to him through what we have learned to call his hypostatic union with the Godhead, he entered into that heart of darkness – the 'belly of the whale' – in apparent alienation from the Father in relation to whom his whole being was defined. The willingness of the only Son to endure this horror for our salvation turned out, however, to be the re-affirmation of his unique bond with the Father. His supreme act of sacrifice allowed the Father to make the humanity of Jesus the vehicle for the endless outpouring of his Spirit on all flesh. At Easter and Pentecost each year we celebrate that one mystery with the two faces: the resurrection of the Son and the sending forth of the Spirit by whom charity is spread abroad in our hearts and we are able to cry out, *Abba*, Father!, as God's adopted children.

4

The Rose in the Crown

'...born of the Virgin Mary...'

There is no rose of such virtue
As is the rose that bear Jesu:
Allelulia.

Heaven and earth in little space:
Res miranda.

By that rose we may well see
There be one God in Persons Three:
Pares forma.

The angels sang, the shepherds too:
Gloria in excelsis Deo:
Gaudeamus.

Leave we all this worldly mirth
And follow we this joyful birth:
Transeamus.

EXTRAORDINARY as it is to relate, there are some
Christians who think no more of the Mother of Christ than
of the donkey that carried him into Jerusalem. This has
been a blind spot of much Protestantism. How Catholics
understand Mary, like how they understand her Son, is
often best exemplified by the way they celebrate the
principal events of her existence *vis-à-vis* God.

The Immaculate Conception

Christians have never thought of blessed Mary as just an ordinary Palestinian lass. The orthodox Fathers held a high doctrine of the divine motherhood and never associated serious personal sin – freely choosing what is morally evil – with one who was the dwelling-place of the Father's only-begotten Son, the Ark where the divine Presence came to tabernacle. On the other hand, it was not plain to Catholic divines, especially in the West, how exactly the Mother of God could be said to be free from all the consequences of the Fall – could be all-holy from the first moment of her existence – without compromising the claim that Jesus Christ saves universally, a claim which surely implies that all men and women without exception need salvation.

The Franciscan theological tradition showed the way out of this impasse. If the Saviour really redeems us absolutely, if he can redeem utterly, perfectly, then there must be at any rate one human being who is absolutely, utterly, perfectly, redeemed – one human being who can demonstrate that being transformed by grace is a real possibility for the rest of us. This person will need, accordingly, to be liberated from sin from the word 'Go'. He or she will exemplify the way God in Jesus Christ can redeem us perfectly, *right down to the very roots of our being*. And there is no difficulty about identifying who answers to that description. This is what the instinct of faith has always wanted to say about Mary, heaping up praises of her faith, purity, holiness, in an effort (we can now see) to bring precisely this intuition to expression.

The first of the mysteries of Mary has a clear application to the rest of us. If God in Jesus Christ can so redeem as he did in Mary, then he really can change us as well! The Immaculate Conception confronts us with the most full-blooded salvational realism – the mighty power of God to transfigure his human creation – as no other aspect of our faith can. On the feast of the Immaculate Conception we celebrate not only our Lady, but in her and with her the whole Church's hope of becoming holy and immaculate in all its members. All sanctity has a relation to the Immaculate in the unique fullness of her sharing in her Son's redemptive sacrifice and its fruit, the reconciled and risen life. That is how for Hilaire Belloc a holy woman known to him could be Mary's copy.

> ... as you pass, the natural life of things
> Proclaims the Resurrection: as you pass
> Remembered summer shines across the grass
> And somewhat in me of the immortal sings.
> You were not made for memory, you are not
> Youth's accident I think but heavenly more;
> Moulding to meaning my pen's poor blot
> And opening wide that long forbidden door
> Where stands the Mother of God, your exemplar.
> How beautiful, how beautiful you are!

The childhood of the Virgin

Evidently, if Mary lived, she was born. The Church, however, has more to ponder today on the feast of Mary's nativity than just a logical entailment. The birth of the Virgin opens up two perspectives. The liturgy looks first to the past, to the Old Testament which makes up the history of Mary's people, summed up in the genealogy, her family tree. Through Mary, the Christ Child is rooted in this very human soil. Through her the promises generated by Jewish history can point to him, and, as we have seen, a knowledge of these promises is prerequisite for a grasp of her person and work. So Mary links the Old Covenant to the New, introducing each into the other. But second, the liturgy also looks to the future, the future destiny of Mary's Child, acclaiming her – in the words of an ancient Latin hymn, the *Ave Maris Stella* – as 'the Gate through which the Light was poured', the departure-point of our salvation.

In the Church's memory, Mary was dedicated to God's service from her earliest years. When invited to be Mother of the Messiah, the answer she will give reflects a formed intention of perpetual virginity. Jewish texts witness to the conviction that contact with the Shekinah – the dwelling place of the divine Glory – involved abstention from sexual activity (to approach the Glory appropriately takes all one's powers of self-donation). So Mary's virginity puts her in a condition fit for overshadowing by that Glory of the Lord. According to an early Christian tradition, her parents brought her to the Jerusalem temple, centre of Israel's worship, as a sign of her consecration to the 'angelic' life. But the life of the angels is also a life of mission, of being at God's disposal, with a view to succouring others who need help on the way of salvation. At the Annunciation, Mary will place herself in the service not only of the Lord (though that first and foremost) but of all those who were awaiting the redemption of Israel.

The Annunciation

A moment that not only changed the world, but, more than that, the relation between the world and God. No surprise then that the Gospel describes Mary as 'much perplexed' (Lk 1:29) at the angelic salutation. Only a great novelist who was also a convinced theological realist could do any sort of justice to the occasion in prose. But there are many artists who have done just that in terms of form and colour. One thinks of Duccio's *Annunciation* with its daring portrayal of Mary's physical recoil, as in initial fear she shields herself with her cloak while holding in her hand the text of Israel's sacred writings open at the page of Isaiah's prophecy of a Virgin who will carry 'Emmanuel', God-with-us. Many people have said 'Yes' to God in various circumstances. But none like this.

Mary's consent is all-important. In taking flesh in a human mother's womb God could not violate his creature, for that would transgress the most basic Creator–creature relationship. So in the Annunciation he turns to Mary, appealing to her will, waiting (though not for long) for her reply. Again, this particular mother had to be capable of introducing her Child, as man, into the fullness of Israel's religion, which was the already existing divine revelation to mankind and so would form the indispensable background to Jesus' mission. And lastly, the matrix into which the Logos entered when he stepped into the created material realm had to be perfectly disposed to union with himself. If modern psychology has any glimmerings of truth at all, there can be no perfect son without a perfect mother – and this the Immaculate (she alone!) could be.

> It all hangs on the fiat. If her fiat was the Great Fiat, nevertheless, seeing the solidarity, we participate in the fiat – or can indeed, by our fiats – it stands to reason. Not chosen and forechosen of Theos Soter [God the Saviour], indeed, but not so jealous, sisters: there are proportions and magnitudes and degrees both of conferrings and of acceptances, very and many various, and, after all, sisters, he was her *baban* [baby].

The Visitation

Catholics most commonly think of Our Lady in connection with God the Son who as man is the fruit of her womb – that, evidently, is the message of the feasts of the Annunciation and Christmas. They also think of her in relation to God the Father, who chose her from all eternity – the message of the feasts of her Immaculate Conception and Nativity. But there is also the question of her relation to God the Holy Spirit whom the gospel of the Annunciation festival describes as 'overshadowing' her (Lk 1:35) with his transforming presence. It is lest we forget this aspect of her mystery that the Church gives us the feast of the Visitation (2 July – Old

Calendar; 31 May – New). In the gospel of the day (Lk 1:39-56), it is when her cousin Elizabeth hears Mary's greeting that she is filled with the Holy Spirit. Although as God the Holy Spirit is immediately related to each and every person, none the less it is when Elizabeth enters into contact with Mary that he is passed on to the cousin of the Virgin in this incarnate way. One way we celebrate, in the season after Pentecost, the Father's sending of the Spirit through the Son, is to honour the effect of that sending in the person of Mary – that effect which renders her an icon of the Spirit's action. Just before his death, Jesus tells the disciples that he will not leave them orphaned – comfortless, desolate, afflicted (Jn 14:18). But Jesus could not be said to have kept that promise if Christians never received any religious *mothering*. It is part of the evangelical experience that the Holy Spirit works to mother us, and, we add as Catholics, does so precisely through Mary. The cult of Mary as 'Mother of the Church' is all to do with the Holy Spirit. The Holy Spirit is the 'Paraclete', our gracious Advocate, and we say the same of Mary in the ancient Latin antiphon, the *Salve Regina*. The Spirit is Comforter of the afflicted, and so, according to her litany, is Mary. The Spirit comes to our aid in our weakness, and the same litany calls Mary the 'help of Christians'. We might even venture the speculation that as Christ is the image of the Father so – in a way proper to one who remains simply human as we are – is Mary of the Holy Spirit. But all this is hidden in the mystery of the Visitation, and only disclosed on her Assumption, when she joins her Son in glory and takes on the task of a universal intercession expanding to the dimensions of the Spirit's own.

During the public ministry

Mary's role in the public ministry of Jesus seems at first sight a negative one. Such moments as: losing the child Jesus in the Temple (Lk 2:41-50); the apparent rebuke she receives at the Wedding Feast of Cana (Jn 2:1-11); the seeming 'put-down' when he declares his *real* mother to be whoever does the will of the heavenly Father (Mt 12:50, and parallels), have all been seen by much Protestant exegesis as indicators of a 'low' Mariology in the Gospels. Certainly, the attempt to show that these rebuffs are actually quite complimentary seems not especially persuasive. I prefer the view which sees these episodes as genuine 'distancings' of Jesus from Mary where, however, the Son invites the Mother to enter with him that experience of abandonment which will come to its climax at the Cross. In happenings outwardly negative, superlatively positive activity is inwardly at work. The Son is transforming his Mother's faith from being the faith of Israel (though the faith of Israel in uniquely fulfilled form) into being a 'cruciform' faith, a faith of the kind that will typify the Church. Precisely by turning away from her, he teaches her the demands of his mission and what is going to be her share in the mission of that Church she will personally embody. He shows her the way her *fiat* will have to endure through darkness and incomprehension. And this lays the foundation for the Mother's future collaboration with the Son's atoning deed, her 'co-redemption'.

The Co-redemption

At the Cross the Church was brought into being precisely as *Holy* Church in the person of our Lady. She, the elect daughter of Zion, was the one in whom the Synagogue, Israel, became the *Ecclesia*, the Bride of Christ. As Newman wrote to E. B. Pusey, Anglican critic of Catholic attitudes to Mary, no one would have spoken of the Church as glorious and venerable unless it was so in *someone*. The Church – as a personality distinct from her personnel, her members (that is a distinction I shall return to in chapter 7), was immediately embodied in her first and pre-eminent member, the Mother of the Lord. That gives Mary a unique role to play at the climax of the redemptive action, and it is something the Tradition links to 'compassion', her co-suffering with the Son she so painfully offered to the Father as she saw him die. The English Victorian priest–theologian Frederick William Faber comments:

It was His ordinance that her compassion should lie close by his Passion and that his Passion without her compassion would be a different passion from what it actually was.

Which points us to the truth that (still in Faber's words), 'All the mysteries of Jesus and Mary were in God's design as one mystery'. All Catholic understanding of and devotion to Mary pans out, consciously or not, from this central intuition. Here what we are concerned with is the way Mary's apparent uselessness at the foot of the Cross concealed its own opposite. What was actually happening was that she was becoming the womb in which the dying incarnate Word was placing the seed of the Church. (He says to the beloved disciple standing by, 'Here is your mother!' [Jn 19:27].) The whole fruitfulness – the total transformative power – of the Church began at that moment in Mary's consent to the redemptive sacrifice. In our Lady the Church herself, then, consented to the Redemption and continues to consent in, with, and through Mary's never retracted Yes to the death of her Son, such that redemption not only once upon a time but ever afterwards passes through Mary. St Thomas meets in advance the Protestant objection that this derogates from the all-sufficient mediation of Christ:

Christ alone is the perfect Mediator between God and man, inasmuch as he reconciled mankind with God by his death... but there is nothing to prevent others in a certain way from being called mediators between God and man insofar as they, by preparing or serving (*dispositive vel ministerialiter*), cooperate in uniting men to God.

The Assumption

When the dogma of the Assumption was promulgated in 1950, it was welcomed in some unlikely quarters – by the psychologist Carl Gustav Jung, for example. It was also, and more predictably, ridiculed in others. Was it not a belated addition to Christianity – hot off the production line of the papal fact factory, as one Anglican theologian (Austin Farrer) put it? And yet the Liturgy had been proclaiming for long enough the doctrine that Mary's taking up into heaven was an integral part of the Gospel claims. For centuries, in East and West alike, the faithful had celebrated this mystery. At this high-point of her existence, the texts of the Western Mass and Office had applied to our Lady the marvelling words of the bridegroom in the Song of Songs:

> Who is this that looks forth like the
>   rising dawn,
> Fair as the moon, bright as the sun,
>   terrible as an army with banners? (6:10)

As was observed at the time of the papal definition of the Assumption, feathers stayed unruffled as long as the answer to this question remained, 'Nobody in particular'. For everyone can appreciate the *general archetypal pattern* found in images of the Assumption: son reunited with mother, father with daughter, spirit with matter. Artists have drawn on this to convey a sense of balance, completeness and repose. Something like the same configuration can be found in many cultures untouched by Christianity – as in China, where the union of the male and female principles was regarded as the manifestation of the ultimate wisdom, and the goal of the human way. The paganising alchemists of the Renaissance made the Assumption the symbol of their own quest: a mystical redemption through the transformation of matter. All this we can appreciate, or if it be fanciful and foreign, it is at least not a shock. What by contrast *is* shocking to us is the claim that the body of a first century Jewess was taken by God to be with him for ever. Here we encounter in a fresh form that 'scandal of particularity' which must necessarily attach to a religion based on the incarnation of the Creator.

St Paul, preaching to Athenian philosophers, got on beautifully so long as he confined himself to generalities. But then he made a tactical mistake: he shifted tack to the resurrection of Jesus Christ. As the Acts of the Apostles relates, Paul was courteously but firmly moved on. They would be delighted to hear more – but not just now. Philosophers struggling to divest themselves of popular religiosity so as to reach an understanding of the transcendence of the divine principle over against everything in the world, were not going to embrace the myth of a dying and rising god, still less to accept that the myth had become fact in the body of a certain Jesus of Nazareth. Yet Paul's tactical mistake was unavoidable since it corresponded with God's strategy: the transfiguration of our flesh by its taking-up into his life. Only under new conditions of embodiment, opening out from history by divine power, is real redemption feasible. And Catholic Christians find it unthinkable that the woman who bore the eternal Word in her body and stood by him (literally and metaphorically) in his world-redeeming activity should not – before all others – have been herself redeemed and share his Glory.

Ultimate Sacrifice

'*... suffered under Pontius Pilate, was crucified, dead and buried; he descended into hell; the third day he rose again from the dead; he ascended into heaven, sitteth at the right hand of the Father; from thence he shall come to judge the living and the dead...*'

> Rise, heir of fresh eternity
>   From thy virgin tomb;
> Rise, mighty man of wonders, and thy
>   world with thee,
>   Thy tomb, the universal east,
>   Nature's new womb,
> Thy tomb, fair immortality's perfumed nest.
>
> Of all the glories make noon gay
>   This is the morn.
> This rock buds forth the fountain of the
>   streams of day.
>   In joy's white annals live this hour
>   When life was born;
> No cloud scowl on his radiant lids, no
>   tempest lower.
>
> Life, by this light's nativity,
>   All creatures have.
> Death only by this day's just doom is forced to die:
>   Nor is death forced; for may he lie
>   Throned in thy grace:
> Death will on this condition be content to die.

FOR man to play the tyrant over against other men is no surprise, as history tells. For God to play the tyrant over human beings is no doubt what many people, ignorant of the nature of the divine 'fathering' of creation would take for granted. But that man should play the tyrant over against One who was God, and a better man than anyone else, ought to produce in us a sense of dramatic shock. This is certainly news, and, as we shall see, *good* news ('Gospel'), and indeed the best of news.

At the Last Supper, Jesus ordered his disciples to celebrate the new covenant to be made between God and humankind in his blood, by a sacramental representation of his sacrificial death. (There will be more to say about the Mass in chapter 8.) Equipped with this rite, for as long as the ordeal lasted they would themselves be the eschatological temple in its earthly aspect, the house built on rock which the power of Hades would try in vain to overcome. The Church, which the disciples constituted in relation to Jesus, would be the mystery of the kingdom, the reign of God, the day of the Son of Man, in so far as that kingdom, reign, day – terms for the new epoch of saving grace – are already manifested in time. Until the definitive ingathering of the saved at the end of time (the plenary coming of the new heaven and the new earth), the redemptive purposes of Jesus would be continued and incorporated in this community.

Having instituted the sacrificial meal of his own memorial and sung a hymn, the Messiah went out with his friends onto the Mount of Olives (more precisely, into a garden just across the Cedron, on its lower slopes, an olive orchard where the Gethsemane church stands today). After his agony, endured while the disciples largely slept, noises and lights announced the arrival of the betrayer. The rest, as they say, is history.

Dying to know us

When the Church affirms that it was *for us* that the incarnate Son suffered and died what she intends first and foremost to say is that he *took our place*. He changed places with us. The Father made the One who knew no sin to 'be sin, so that in him we might become the right-eousness of God' (2 Cor 5:21). He became what we are so that we might become what he is. The sinless Son put himself in the situation of sinners so that they could be re-situated as sons in the Son, and so 'close to the Father's heart' – which is where the Prologue to St John's Gospel (Jn 1:18) declares the Son's place to be. For St Paul, the Son took on himself the weight of our guilt so that we might enjoy the glorious liberty of the sons of God. In the Incarnation he had already – by an 'admirable exchange', as the Roman liturgy puts it – taken on himself the poverty of our humanity so that we might become rich with his divinity (cf. 2 Cor 8:9). Now, in the atonement he confirms that exchange by a climactic dramatic gesture which con-stitutes the turning-point of the whole history of God with man and man with God.

Not that the mystery of the Cross can be reduced to a single formula. St Thomas Aquinas – hardly an opponent of lucid formulations – is insistent that no one concept can subsume that mystery. The act of atonement was:

– the all-sufficient Sacrifice – a representative, substi-tutionary act of satisfaction, where the demands of both mercy and justice are reconciled, for the sins of the whole world;

– and so the disclosure of the divine compassion and philanthropy or loving-kindness towards men;

– but also victory over death and hell;

– and therefore the ultimate icon of the holy and life-giving Trinity;

- and so the perfect act of worship, the foundation for a new and definitive cultic order for man the worshipping animal;
- and the vehicle for the Blessed Trinity's endless outreach, through the Church, into the world.

So what was done on the Cross had a multidimensional nature, though all proceeded from the unconditional triune love. But as the title of the present chapter indicates, its *sacrificial character* is primary, and gives us a key to unlock the rest.

Only because Christ is God, only because he is infinitely all-embracing, do his human sufferings have an inclusiveness about them that enables them in so varied a fashion to affect the condition of the world. His uniqueness as the God-man – the man who is God – is the ground of his relationship to all human beings as their Head, the Second Adam. Only because he is both God and man is Christ able to substitute himself vicariously for us, to take on himself the otherwise unbearable weight of the guilt of all the world. Only someone who is One of the Holy Trinity can, as man, die 'for all'. There is, too, a peculiar fittingness about the fact that the Trinitarian Person who did so die was specifically the Logos, through whom, as various New Testament hymns (most explicitly Jn 1:1-18) have it, all things came to be. Since he was the universal Word through whom, in whom and for whom all things were made, he was able to communicate to the human nature united to his own Person something of his divine universality – without, however, robbing that human nature of its particularity. And this prepares us for the discovery that his reconciling action on Calvary is not only something exclusive to him. It is that, but it is also something inclusive of ourselves, of the whole human race. The sinless God-man acts exclusively in doing what only he can do, but he acts inclusively in standing in for us as our Head. 'Sinless': that is important, because divinely absolute innocence, humanly embodied, is of the essence of the atonement's antidote to sin. Sin is, in some respect or another, self-enclosure. It is a hindrance, and often a crippling one, to self-outpouring love. So a sinful self-substituting Redeemer would be a contradiction in terms. Moreover, the Saviour's quintessential vulnerability – typical of a Trinitarian Person who only exists *in* his relationships and thus by giving himself away – is also key to his capacity to be our representative substitute. Whereas sinful human beings can always shield themselves by growing a protective shell, the divine Son, even in his human state, is utterly incapable of following this example. Thanks to its union with his (literally!) selfless divine Person, the human heart of Christ is necessarily vulnerable to the total limit. It is absolutely incapable of non-compassion.

This makes his experience of the state of sin deeper and darker than ours could ever be. The suffering of Christ is, then, primarily spiritual but his physical torments can be seen as a sort of perverse sacrament of his spiritual agony. Still, since the saving substitution on the Cross manifests not the Father's will to punish the guilty but the triune love, all these events of the Passion serve only to display the mutual engagement of Father and Son in the Holy Spirit. In his love for the Father the Son wants to renew the Father's fallen creation, while the Father, in sending the Son into the world once made through him, wants all things to be reconciled and integrated in the Person of the Son. The mediaeval English alabasters which portray the Father holding out the Crucified, the Spirit of their love hovering between them, are called – not for nothing – 'Thrones of Mercy'. On the other hand, the New Testament also has a language of divine wrath. True, the love of God is the Church's supreme message – but it is a terrible, a demanding, love she proclaims (precisely for our benefit), not some declaration about a celestial 'sugar-daddy' who can always be relied on as a soft touch (and thus leave us as, regrettably, we are). In allowing himself to be given up, the Son abandons himself to the dreadful impact of the Father's total negation of sin. That awful fire that is the Father's love can only burn whatever is loveless. (That is relevant to the imagery of Purgatory. In Newman's *The Dream of Gerontius*, the angel-guardian tells the soul on its way to judgement, 'Learn that the Flame of the Everlasting Love doth burn ere it transform'.) In what the English lay-theologian John Saward has punningly called 'that crossfire', the Trinity is superlatively laid bare as a communion of love.

The ultimate surprise about the Cross is that the Father's very abandonment of the Son is what reveals the unity of substance between them, the union of the Persons in the divine being. It is the work of the Holy Spirit, the enabler of Christian faith, to make that known. The Father and the Son glorify each other on the Cross, from where the Spirit is sent. It is through his docility to the Holy Spirit that the Son, now not only incarnate but crucified, allows the Father's love for the world to burn up the human evil which is despoiling it, an evil he now bears in concentrated form in his own humanly realised Person. And the most typical result of that redeeming action will be the creation of the Church as itself a communion that images the Blessed Trinity. In the life of the redeemed, estrangement from others – where we differ from each other in a vicious way, a way that generates spite and conflict – yields to 'good otherness', the otherness of love where I can rejoice in the difference of others and so enter into communion with them without threat to my own identity. The Church of the Holy Spirit will be a communion in the likeness of the divine life.

And so the Cross is the true axle of the world. In Giovanni Bellini's *The Blood of the Redeemer*, Christ appears as himself the Sacrifice to end all sacrifices, superseding the pagan libations and worship to polytheistic gods shadowily depicted on *bas-reliefs* behind him. His blood flows in a perpetual stream from the wound in his right side – the wound closest to his heart – into the Eucharistic chalice, as he bares his body to our gaze as the merciful relief for our condition, the living Bread come down from heaven to give life to the world (cf. Jn 6:51). Or, as an image in the church of St Lawrence at Nuremberg would have it, his Cross fruits, bearing grapes – a reference to the sacraments, which for Catholics are vehicles of the life-giving Passion, encounters with the Sacrificed Lamb. In the words of Cardinal Roger Etchegaray:

> The royal door by which the love of God gushes forth upon us is that of the heart of his Son, pierced on the cross. Here is the holy door, the door of jubilation.

The blood of Christ seals a new and everlasting covenant whereby the Trinitarian life flows out into the world – not, however, before it has in Christ descended into hell.

The Descent into Hell

In the Passion of Christ the Enemy of our race was overthrown. The Lamb fought, and conquered. Since to understand these statements fully would mean grasping sheerly evil intelligence and will in their essence, we are fortunate not to know entirely what these words mean. But when the Apostles' Creed speaks of Christ's 'descent into hell', it has something else in view. The descent of the Logos does not end in the Flesh-taking, simply by his becoming man. As a hymn embedded in St Paul's Letter to the Philippians has it, 'And being found in human form, he humbled himself…'(2:7-8), becoming obedient not only to the death on the Cross but lower still. He descended to that nadir of human fortunes the Hebrew Bible calls *Sheol*, the dead end of human wretchedness beyond the grave. Our compassionate High Priest wanted to have first-hand experience not only of our dying but also of our being dead. St Thomas Aquinas says, the Word willed to share all the disabilities of sinners, sin itself apart. He who is the foundation of all communication – only think of the word 'Word' – entered in his humanly ensouled Person a state of total speechlessness, which was the most eloquent proclamation of the Father's love for us there could possibly be.

The effect of Christ's presence in this silent, lonely world of the departed was electric. Taken in conjunction with his Resurrection and Ascension, the transformation he works turns *Sheol* into its opposite, the indestructible communion of the holy souls in Purgatory, and of the blessed in Heaven. At the same time the Descent, by leaving in its wake the logical possibility that someone may reject this divine love which went down into the depths for their sake, also creates the real possibility of eternal damnation. For damnation is saying 'No' definitively to all that love can do.

The Resurrection

It was in his Virgin-born body, scourged, nailed, pierced and laid in the tomb that the Lord rose – a body changed in state but not in nature. To suppose that Christ rose in his soul alone, or in the faith of his disciples only, or by some sort of 'replacement' body, is to imply, for the Logos, the reversal of true Incarnation. It is to allege that the divine economy climaxed in a lie. Not of course that the Resurrection means only transfigured biology for the body of Jesus. That would be strikingly unusual, but hardly *the* event against which all other events in nature and history are to be measured. To indicate something of its dimensions we need recourse, once again, to the Trinitarian Persons for this is their supreme (as yet) interaction with the world.

– The Resurrection is the *Father*'s acceptance of the Son's sacrifice. It is the culmination of the Father's work as the Creator, for here the Father shows himself faithful to the original covenant of creation and all its renewals in Israel's history. By means of the Resurrection he displays the Son to the world as its *Pantokrator,* its 'All-ruler', thus fulfilling the prayer Jesus made on the eve of his Passion, 'Father, glorify me in your own presence with the glory that I had in your presence before the world existed' (Jn 17:5). In thus receiving its Lord the world is immeasurably enhanced, for it is drawn up into that communication of love going on for ever in the Holy Spirit between Father and Son.

– At the Resurrection it is in the *Spirit* that the Father raises the Son, and in that way the Spirit brings the world to its goal. Just as the head is inseparable from the body, so the Spirit now overflows from the glorified manhood of the Second Adam, humanity's new head, onto his corporate body, the disciples of his Church.

– The Resurrection is the validation of the *Son*'s claims, the establishment of the Kingdom. The risen body of the Saviour becomes the nucleus of a new creation. In the forty days that separate the first Easter from the Ascension, the Son provides for his friends the abiding archetypal experience of that Church. As the risen Christ shows himself to his friends in a way both homely and marvellous, earthly time – the time of the Church after Pentecost – is also time filled with bliss, with the serene confidence that flows from the victory over sin and death. The sacramental life of the Church will share these two interrelated characteristics – earthliness combined with the reign of sovereign grace.

The Ascension and Session

The Ascension of Christ brings history into the service of the End, the ultimate goal of the Creator's plan. It involves a real departure by Jesus who will be henceforth 'in' the Father – a human 'he', now present in the Trinitarian Source with all his concrete physical and temporal particularity preserved, yet collapsing its limits, so that from now on the Glory is thrown open through him to the world. We should not allow ourselves to be so bemused by the reports of the disappearing feet that we either over-literalise the Ascension or deny the real difference it makes to space–time. The mediaeval English author of *The Cloud of Unknowing* wrote:

> Since it was so that Christ should ascend bodily, and thereafter send the Holy Ghost bodily, therefore it was more seemly that it was upwards and from above than either downwards and from beneath, behind, or before, on one side or on another. But else than for this seemliness, he needed never the more to have gone upwards than downwards; I mean for nearness of the way. For heaven ghostly is as near down as up, and up as down, behind as before, before as behind, on one side as on other.

And when the *Cloud* author adds that 'the high and the nearest way thither is run by desires, and not by paces of feet', he knows perfectly well that to 'go to heaven ghostly', by love and desire, is not yet to go bodily – else we should have at the Father's right hand a disembodied Christ. But no. The Ascension makes the End something in the largest sense sacramental – bodily, tangible, thick with the precious stuff of this world.

Space and time, nature and history, have now entered the Trinity, and the world will never be the same again. That fusion of earth and heaven Jesus called the Kingdom has happened, and history is on course, in his Covenant, in his Church, to a very different end from what the general story of culture and politics might suggest. One who can claim the inheritance not only of Israel but of Adam enters the presence of the Ancient of Days, there to receive dominion over all things for their everlasting welfare. That claim to universal lordship of the Crucified is well attested in the 'palindrome' (a series of letters so arranged that they read identically whether up or down, backwards or forwards) found inscribed on a Spanish amphora of about the year 185, and now preserved in the Manchester Museum.

ROTAS
OPERA
TENET
AREPO
SATOR

That is, 'The Sower [*sator*, i.e. Christ who sows the seed], at the plough [*arepo*, on the Cross], holds [*tenet*], with his sacrifice [*opera*], the wheels [*rotas*, of destiny or history]'.

This implies the Session, the 'seating' at the Father's right hand. To mediate the fulfilment of creation, the Son enters into all power. He will use it only redemptively – in both covenanted and uncovenanted ways: *covenanted,* to enable the Church to teach the world truth, to sanctify the creation and bring it to the Father; *uncovenanted,* to act invisibly on human hearts in the process of world history, in a way known to God alone.

The Parousia of the Spirit and the Son

'Parousia' is a Greek word that means presence or coming. It signifies in the first place the *moral outcome* of the ultimate sacrifice for us as free agents before God. Jesus Christ is not only the Saviour, he is also the Judge who will test heart and reins, searching not only the outward act but the inner motive. He is Saviour in that he judges with mercy, but mercy is far from being indulgence or he would not also be Judge. He brings to bear on the behaviour of human beings the ultimate criterion of all human agency, the sacrificial love of the Cross.

He does this initially at Pentecost, when he sends the Holy Spirit as the Spirit of judgement, to convict the world of sin, but also as the Paraclete, the Advocate, who pleads for guilty humanity on the basis of Christ's redeeming blood.

By his own word, Christ promises to come again, however, in his own divine–human Person, not invisibly as in the Pentecost Parousia of the Spirit but visibly, to show the world its crucified Judge.

But here morals are not to be separated from metaphysics. The twofold advent of Spirit and Son – Pentecost and the Second Coming with the Final Judgement and the General Resurrection will incorporate the human world – the souls of the living and the dead, and the material cosmos that is their integument, into his Reign – except where the peace his completed Sacrifice won is rejected, and violence and cruelty re-affirmed. He offers life for death, but created liberty will still be free – one last time – to return, in a hideous parody of his saving work, death for life.

Gracious Spirit

'... in the Holy Ghost...'

Creator Spirit, by whose aid
The World's Foundations first were laid,
Come visit ev'ry pious Mind;
Come pour thy Joys on Human Kind:
From Sin, and Sorrow set us free;
And make thy Temples worthy Thee.

O, Source of uncreated Light,
The Father's promis'd *Paraclite*!
Thrice Holy Fount, Thrice Holy Fire,
Our hearts with Heav'nly Love inspire;
Come, and thy Sacred Unctions bring
To Sanctifie us, while we sing!

Plenteous of Grace, descend from high,
Rich in thy sev'n fold Energy!
Thou Strength of his Almighty Hand,
Whose Pow'r does Heav'n and Earth command:
Proceeding Spirit, our Defence,
Who dos't the Gift of Tongues dispense,
And crown'st thy Gift, with Eloquence!

Refine and purge our Earthy Parts;
But, oh, inflame and fire our Hearts!
Our Frailties help, our Vice controul;
Submit the Senses to the Soul;
And when Rebellious they are grown,
Then, lay thy hand, and hold 'em down.
Chace from our Minds th'Infernal Foe;
And Peace, the fruit of Love, bestow:

And, lest our Feet shou'd step astray,
Protect, and guide us in the way.

Make us Eternal Truths receive,
And practise, all that we believe:
Give us thy self, that we may see
The Father and the Son, by thee.

Immortal Honour, endless Fame
Attend th'Almighty Father's Name:
The Saviour Son, be glorify'd,
Who for lost Man's Redemption dy'd:
And equal Adoration be
Eternal *Paraclete*, to thee.

Who is the Spirit?

THE Holy Spirit was already known to be (in the words of
the Great Creed) 'the Lord, the Giver of Life' in the Old
Testament where he appears as the Spirit by which God
acts in creating man, 'enspiriting' him and inspiring various
kinds of activity – political in the Book of Judges, artistic
in the Book of Exodus, literary in the oracles of the prophets.
(Interestingly, all of these require a combination of creative
flair with disciplined order.) In the Hebrew Bible, the Spirit
might seem to be no more than a *mode* of divine action. But
in the Gospels, it is made clear that he proceeds from the
Father and the Son – in other words, that he enjoys a distinct
personal identity which comes across unmistakably via
the work of Christ. Of course, he is still the One who 'has
spoken through the prophets'. He is not a different Person
from the Spirit of the Lord known to our Israelite fathers in
faith. Yet now, with the Pentecostal overflow of the grace
abounding of the Crucifixion, Resurrection and Ascension,
he operates by means of a new 'economy'. Suddenly a new
pattern of saving activity allowed that distinctive Personhood
of his to come through loud and clear. We also add in the
Creed of Nicaea–Constantinople that 'with the Father and

the Son he is 'worshipped and glorified'. That is the Church's way of saying that the Spirit is really and truly God. She puts it thus because in her liturgy – the primary setting for the recitation of the Creed – we do not make bare assertions in a clinically cold frame of mind, but prayerful, adoring ones in a warmly responsive one. How could the Spirit *not* be divine if all the godly qualities that people begin to acquire under his shaping influence are taken into account:

– regeneration of the spiritually and ethically moribund.

– the 'fruits' of the Spirit listed by St Paul in his pen-picture of the typical Christian personality: love, joy, peace, patience, kindness, goodness, faithfulness, gentleness, self-control (Gal 5:22-23).

– or the gifts of the Spirit which take the Christian into the higher reaches of the mystical life, more sensitively attuned to the presence of the Father and the Son, in the neighbour, the cosmos, and the depths of the soul.

In the Holy Spirit, God acts directly upon us; in giving us the Holy Spirit he gives us himself. In the Spirit the Father reaches out to us for redemptive, sanctifying ends, to bring us, healed, restored, forgiven into communion with the endlessly beneficent Source. Just as the Son could not save unless he fully shared the being and agency that is the Father's, so too with the Spirit. Divinising can only be done by One who is divine.

Spirituality

As his name suggests, the Spirit is the medium of Catholic spirituality, a series of ways, joined by family likeness, in which people love God thanks to God's own love 'poured into our hearts through the Holy Spirit that has been given to us' (Rom 5:5). All the authentic spirituality of the Church begins at Pentecost, when the light and fire of the Holy Spirit was not just visibly symbolised in the flames

85

appearing above the heads of the twelve apostles, the Mother of God in their midst, but also descended invisibly into the hearts of these first of all believers. *Contemplation* was at the start of the Church, and its remains her true centre. The seventeenth-century Benedictine spiritual theologian Augustine Baker points out in his *Confessions* that the first knowledge of the Christian mysteries 'came in and by contemplations... to which God called the holy apostles, doctors and other principal members and beginners of the Church', and was then 'imparted to other Christians who took it by tradition from those contemplators who saw and felt the truth of those mysteries'. Contemplation and the experience of divine realities is our chief way of making progress in the understanding of that world of revelation which this small book invites its readers to enter. The mystical life is not an extraordinary gift of the 'gracious Spirit': Christians may share in it to varying degrees even at the outset of the life of faith, hope and charity which is theirs. From gentle beginnings, prayer grows in intensity as the desire for God becomes ardent yearning for him. As the knowledge and love of God are purified and deepened, periods of emptiness alternate with moments of delight. These encounters happen in a 'place' which lies beyond the senses, but their blessing brims over into the emotions. Then by the mystical touch – contact with his uncreated triune Substance – God wounds the soul with love, giving it a taste of the Life everlasting. This pierces the soul through, and makes it burn with thirst for him, long to see him face to face in the final vision. 'It is heaven', writes Blessed Elizabeth of the Trinity, 'that the Holy Spirit creates in you' (Letter 239).

As human beings we are language-using animals. Consequently, vocal prayer is the most natural to us, and indeed it is noble, and can itself be the occasion of perfect contemplation. But we cannot always be vocalising, whereas the true lover *is* always thinking of the beloved. The men and women of the Bible were well aware of a prayer that is song without words, so still is it, so deep. When in the Book of Psalms, the speaker – who represents Israel and the Church – cries out, 'My heart and my flesh sing for joy to the living God!' (84:2), he could find elsewhere in the Psalter the divine reply, 'Be still, and know that I am God' (46:10). We are uncommonly loved by one who never tires of giving. We, then, must not tire of receiving. Notice, however, that he does not give himself completely until we give ourselves completely to him. We are to keep our 'eyes ever toward the LORD' (25:15), to 'behold the beauty of the Lord, to inquire in his temple' (27:4). Almost certainly, this means creating a space for solitude and silence in my life, though once these guests have taken up their abode with me, the soul can take them anywhere. Not speaking is hardly silence in the strong sense contemplation requires. *This* silence is a word that concentrates all words, in love towards the One who said, 'I AM WHO I AM' (Ex 3:14). To hear it one must enter the cave of the heart, the heart's inner chamber.

There is no place here for seeking interesting experiences, or a spiritual sweetness the appetite for which is always self-indulgent and sometimes diabolically sustained. We are not to be occupied in prayer for our own enjoyment, but so as to have the strength to serve. In this sense prayer is altogether practical. As the great Teresa exclaims in a meditation on the Song of Songs,

> Oh, strong love of God! And how true it is
>   that nothing
> seems impossible to one who loves!
>   Oh, happy the soul
> that has obtained this peace from God, for it is master
>   over all
> the trials and dangers of the world.

Since many of those 'trials and dangers' derive from our fellow men and women, the ability to love them effectively despite their vices is not the least of the promises contained in these words. And in fact we can never reach perfection in the love of our neighbour unless that love rises from the love of God as from its root. So when the Spirit gives great graces in contemplation, capturing – captivating! – our faculties of will, imagination, understanding, the proof of the pudding lies in our becoming more skilled in the virtues, bringing forth a richer harvest of that Spirit's fruits.

Grace and freedom

Like the Spirit, the Son is an ethical maximalist. He tells his disciples to be 'perfect, as your heavenly Father is perfect' (Mt 5:48) – a rather tall order, and assures them that unless their righteousness 'exceeds that of the scribes and Pharisees' – sticklers for the moral provisions, among other things, of the Jewish Law – they 'will never enter the kingdom of heaven' (Mt 5:20), they will fail to share in that condition where earth and heaven are fused everlastingly. Suchlike words have to be reconciled, however, with that other teaching of the Saviour, formulated most clearly by St Paul, to the effect that salvation is essentially the gift of God, the result of his freely bestowed mercy. Somehow, then, we have to integrate two truths: first, that we are saved by grace, but second, that our salvation demands from us a strenuous effort if we are to make it our own. If we deny the first, we become Pelagians, people who think you have to save yourself. If we deny the second, we become Antinomians, people who regard the keeping of the moral law as irrelevant to salvation. The Church's doctrine of salvation aims to unify these factors in a satisfactory way. In justification, when we commence, or re-commence, our Christian lives, it is God alone who initiates our salvation, by infusing into us through the Holy Spirit a faith that will be spontaneously fruitful in charity. In sanctification, through which, by the same Spirit, our appropriation of salvation develops, God does not (in St Augustine's words) 'save us without us'. The Holy Spirit delicately adjusts his action to the measure of our capacity to receive him, enabling our freedom to mesh with his continuing gifts of grace. Thus by the kind of perfect charity the saints show in their lives our righteousness may indeed go beyond even the 'righteousness of the scribes and Pharisees' – the best ethical practice of the finest exponents of the true religion, as it existed before the gracious Spirit issued from the ultimate sacrifice made by the One whose fleshtaking was in the rose in the crown.

Our Mother the Church

'*... the holy Catholic Church...*'

Who is She, in candid vesture,
Rushing up from out the brine?
Treading with resilient gesture
Air, and with what Cup divine?
She in us and we in her are,
Beating Godward; all that pine,
Lo, a wonder and a terror –
The Sun hath blushed the Sea to Wine!
He the Anteros and Eros,
She the Bride and Spirit; for
Now the days of promise near us,
And the Sea shall be no more.

What is the Church?

THE Church is the agent of the Holy Spirit in assembling
human beings as the people of God, the Father, and the
body of Christ, his Son. The Apostles' Creed speaks very
succinctly of the consequence – 'I believe in... the holy
Catholic Church' while the Great Creed speaks of all it
involves by doubling the number of adjectives: '*one*, holy,
catholic *and apostolic* Church', for the Spirit of Christ
unifies the Church and preserves her in the faith of the
apostles, as well as hallowing her and making her whole or
universal. In either case, Catholics see the Church as more
of a 'who' than a 'what', and where personal, rather than
impersonal, pronouns are concerned this one must be as
resolutely feminine as our language for God is (special
exceptions apart) resolutely masculine. This is *mother*

Church, who is responsible for our 'birthing' through Christ in the Holy Spirit. The parallel with the Blessed Virgin Mary is obvious – and explains why much of poetry (the citation from Francis Thompson given above is an example) oscillates between the two figures, the Mother of God and Holy Mother Church.

The mystery of the Church, like Mary's intercession, prolongs the missions of both the Logos and the Paraclete, the Son and the Spirit alike. To grasp something of her mystery, we will find ourselves drawing, then, on what the Creed – and well-framed commentary thereon – has to say about both the second and the third Trinitarian Persons, and so inevitably about the first Person, the Father, their common Source. Everything in Catholicism comes back ultimately to the Holy Trinity.

The Church is One

Let us begin with the *unity* of the Church. The unity of the universal Church is something highly prized by Catholics, especially if they have that classic mind-set this little book is trying to reproduce. Not for them the tendency in some quarters today to consider the inner diversity of the Church more important than her unity, to find her differentiation in the form of many local churches each with – at least ideally – its own distinctive life a more *interesting* consideration than the unity of which the Great Creed speaks. Not of course that people deny the unity of the Church, the need to correspond in some way to that note of oneness. But (here the author must allow the reader a glimpse of an internal Catholic debate) they tend to think of the Church's unity as something that is constructed out of the diversity of the many local Catholic churches – the 'dioceses' as, under the influence of the terminology of Roman imperial administration, they came to be known. The Church's unity then becomes an aspect of the inter-relations of these 'particular churches' (the more correct phrase if we are on our theological best behaviour), rather than their prior productive ground. It is absolutely right to seek a generous recognition of the local church's Christian dignity, and of lawful pluralism in thought, worship and cultural life. One would hardly expect, let alone want, the church of Oslo to be a test tube reproduction of the church of Palermo, or the church of Bangkok to be indistinguishable from the church of Bogotà. And yet the Church is not more importantly many than one. She is not equally importantly many and one. Her manifoldness is indisputable but it merits no mention in the Creeds. The reason is the unity of the Father's creating and redeeming plan for the world. It is because the single Father, in sending his only-begotten Son and uniquely spirated Breath (the Spirit) into the world enters upon an all-embracing plan of creation and redemption that there is one and only one Church.

How does the Church manifest the unity the Creed ascribes to her? The Acts of the Apostles describes the unity of the first local church, the church of Jerusalem, in a statement which can serve as a verbal icon for the unity of the Church as a whole.

They devoted themselves to the Apostles' teaching and fellowship, to the breaking of the bread and the prayers (2:42).

The Church's unity is therefore:

– a unity in hearkening to the apostolic preaching, and so a unity in faith. The Church is one because her faith is one, all over the world. In the mediaeval West, the most common sobriquet for the Church was *congregatio fidelium*, 'the assembly of those who have faith'. Faith is that welcoming openness to God's initiative by which we take our stand not on ourselves, first and foremost, but on God's veracity and faithfulness, shown above all in his incarnate Son, and thus enter into his new and everlasting covenant. Such reception of God's Word is unthinkable – literally! – without an intellectual engage-

92

ment on our part. It has to include our conscious reception of fresh understanding, novel certitudes about the purpose of our lives. By faith, then, the members of the Church believe in the same realities, as communicated by the biblical witness and the teaching of the apostles, transmitted through the Church's mission of teaching, which is the prolongation of the apostles' own. Unity of faith unifies the members of the Church *both interiorly and exteriorly*. Interiorly, because, adhering to the same divine Word, the faithful share the same reality as the goal of their Christian understanding – not as an object of knowledge only but as an active Subject who draws them to himself so as to raise their lives to a new supernatural level. Exteriorly, because divine revelation is not given to Christians privately but publicly, and so has mediators who are, or were, publicly accessible: prophets, apostles, the authors and editors of the books in the biblical Canon, the bearers of the magisterium instituted by Christ. These human mediations of faith are never the object of faith: only God is that. Yet they are so bound up with the communication of the divine Word to us that they enjoy a normative value for the faith of the Church. Catholics are keen on authority in religion because they are concerned with solidarity, with brotherhood, with – in a word – *unity* there. And that is only possible if the authentic teaching of the Gospel is available in the form of a corporate rule of faith in the Church. Dogma and the liturgy, once their deliverances are internalised (for like everything that comes from the Incarnation these things work in a human way) unite believers at the highest level. They enable them to share the mind of Christ (nothing less!) – his consciousness of the triune God to whom his human nature was, without either separation or confusion, conjoined, and, along with that, then, his awareness of the Father's saving plan. Mention of the liturgy brings me to the second aspect of the Church's unity highlighted by St Luke, and this is:

– a unity in the offering of prayers and the breaking of bread, and so a unity in cult and the celebration of the sacraments. The Church is bonded together by cultic and (especially) sacramental signs. Faith places us in a 'doxological' – a 'glory-giving' – attitude towards God. The knowledge faith brings is not of an academic kind. It is knowledge of the love for us of the One who is Alpha and Omega, our absolute Beginning and our End. Expressed outwardly, faith naturally takes the form of cult, and cult of its nature has a social character. (One would feel rather silly devising a rite for solo celebration in the bathroom.) Every social manifestation of cult is, for the worshipping group, a principle of unity – unity in the same symbols and gestures (with due respect for the diverse ritual families in Catholicism – Latin, Byzantine, and the rest) and through these in the moulding of awareness, of sensibility. Now the chief component of Catholic worship is the Liturgy of the sacraments where something even more is found. In the sacraments the Church's members are joined not only sociologically or by unity of aim but divinely, by sharing in the supernatural life which flows from these continuations of the work of Christ. Thus the faithful are united by the 'royal priesthood' of Baptism, where they are sacramentally initiated into the covenant of salvation, inaugurated by the Suffering Servant at the Jordan and realised in his own Person at his Easter victory, the Paschal feast. Their union is sealed in the Eucharist, the communion-sacrifice renewing Christ's passing over from death to resurrection whenever it is celebrated. By assimilating the communicants to the *personal* body of the Lord, offered, immolated, raised and glorified, the *sacramental* body of Christ ceaselessly generates his *mystical* body, the Church, sustaining and, where the co-operation of human freedom is forthcoming, deepening her unity. In this sense, the Eucharist 'makes' the Church. It is *the* sacrament of unity. From here it is no great distance to the third sort of unity featured by the Acts of the Apostles:

– a unity in fraternal communion and so in life together. The nature of the Church's social unity differs from that of any other human group. Of course Catholics also belong to other, natural, human groupings – families, circles of friends, neighbourhoods, professional or recreational associations, nation states and the like, so the theologically unique nature of their relations with others *specifically as Catholic Christians* may not always be clear to them. These natural unities complicate the picture, though they can also be taken up into the specific social unity that belongs to the Church. The living charity which typifies the Church as the City of God does not unify in the way other, purely human, agencies can do. It is not a human construct, any more than the Church is another benevolent society. Charity unifies the Church thanks to its source in the Person of the Holy Spirit – to whom the attribute of divine love is especially ascribed owing to his Trinitarian position: he is the bond of love between the Father and the Son. It is in him that we see most clearly how love is a divine forte. The Holy Spirit binds the faithful together by making them participants in the unity of the Trinitarian life. Charity makes the Church a network of mutually assisting agencies, at all levels from a Pope articulating doctrine to a parishioner going to visit someone who is sick. If the Church had a motto it would be, like the Prince of Wales', 'I serve'. But there is not only charity as service, meeting the needs of others. People who have a double dose of moral seriousness can forget charity as communion, simply *enjoying* co-existence with others in God. The Spirit renders the faithful supernaturally open to each other in the communion of saints. In an activist age, in the Church as in the world, it is hard to remember that enjoying co-being with others is the highest form of

95

union with them. If we want to see the charity of the Church figured in sacred art, for instance, we should not look first to Velázquez' delicate study of charity as service in *The Waterseller of Seville,* but at Fra Angelico's *The Blessed in Paradise* or the Byzantine icons called *In You all Creation Rejoices* which show the Church gathered lovingly around the Mother of God. Still, the communion of the faithful has a dimension of public communal interaction which needs to be rightly ordered: this is why the social unity of the Church is also a hierarchical unity. The Church's pastors – in the first place, the Pope and the bishops – take from the apostles their responsibility of overseeing the peace of the Church: the spiritual communion of the faithful, and the mutual services that prompts.

The Church is holy

But we must move on to the *holiness* of the Church. 'Holy Church': a *façon de parler* that is something of a Catholic give-away, as in Newman's poem at the head of the first chapter of this book. For the Church really to be that, she has to be the instrument of the growth in holiness of her members. Christ came to found a new Israel – first fruits of the Kingdom – which would unite people to God, on earth by grace, in heaven by glory. If there *are* sanctifying forces at work in the Church then they come from this. What might they be? They would surely include sacraments, the Scriptures, the doctrines of the Church, the discipline of her common life, the counsels of chastity, poverty, obedience she passes on to monks and nuns and the ethos these represent for people 'in the world' trying to grow in goodness through fulfilling the precepts to love God and neighbour. All these stimulate virtues, shape excellence of character, instil charity. Not, however, if one or other of them is isolated and distorted. Possession of the Scriptures, for instance, might be useless for purposes of growth in

96

holiness if one read the Bible exclusively after the fashion of nineteenth-century source critics or 1960s Structuralists. The Scriptures need to be read in the same Spirit in which they were written if they are to be

> useful for teaching, for reproof, for correction, and for training in righteousness, so that everyone who belongs to God may be proficiently equipped for every good work. (2 Tim 3:16b-17).

All the elements I have mentioned need to function in such a way as to achieve their real end – the holiness of human beings, which is why they are entrusted to the living voice of a Church that knows how actually to make use of them for human salvation.

The litmus test of whether it does any good has to be, of course, in the achieved holiness (if such there be) of the *members* of the Church. Jesus had taught that false prophets will be known by their bitter fruits – their actions, just as a good upstanding human tree can be told by the excellence of the fruit *it* bears. That warning (and encouragement) is echoed in the Letters of St Paul: 'Works of the flesh', unpleasantly symptomatic of fallen humanity, mark out their perpetrators as excluded from the Kingdom; fruits of the Spirit single out those who belong to Christ. Does that mean, then, that holiness has to be visibly realised in each and every member of the Church? Not at all. Jesus also speaks of the scandals his community will endure, as good wheat and tares grow intermingled till the end of the age. Reconciling the two sorts of statement, we can say that *enough* evangelically holy human beings have to be around in the Church for people outside her to find that an interesting enigma – and a sign that the life-resources made available by the Church are out of the ordinary, as they naturally would be if they came from the Word incarnate, Jesus Christ.

I concede, then, that the Church is partially sinful in her members. No one has ever disputed it, the persistence of human frailties among believers is only too apparent. On the first Sunday of Lent in the Jubilee year 2000 Pope John Paul II and leading cardinals of his Curia made a compendious statement of regret for the ills inflicted by even her most highly placed officers. How then can we have the effrontery to say that the Church is none the less indefectibly holy in her essence? As the Holy Spirit creates the Church on the basis of Christ's saving work, he leaves behind in history not only her *personnel* but also her *personality*. The Spirit, by abiding in the Church as one (divine) Person in many (human) persons makes of her a corporate personality to which the word 'holy' can at all times and in all places be unconditionally applied, even when the individual people who belong to her fellowship continue to be manifest – and even *News-of-the-World*-worthy – sinners. The sins which the Church's members commit after aggregation to her unity are not perpetrated by them *qua* members of the Church, *qua* persons who are one flesh with Christ in the Holy Spirit. To say so is not to wriggle off a hook. It is to think through what must be involved in the fact that the Church exists as the personality she is by the same act in which Christ purifies and sanctifies her human members. What should be added, though, is that the holiness of Holy Church is always *repentant* holiness, and this allows us to say that when we repent of our sins, we do that so much as the Church's members that the Church herself can be said to be penitent in us. As our Mother, the Church is penitent for all her sinful members – even those who are not at the present time actually penitent. Notions and practices like: doing penance for the sins of others; exchanging any merits of mine (under grace) for the demerit of others; offering up the fruits of repentance for the conversion of sinners; making reparation for the misdeeds of fellow members in the Body of Christ – all this makes sense because in these ways I can align myself with the personality of the Church as the penitently holy Bride of Christ. And so I can share co-redemptively in the action of Christ in saving sinners (by dependence on his deed, by participation in it).

To say that the Church is essentially holy – that she is brought into being by an act of Christ, through the Holy Spirit, freeing her members from the sin of the world – is not to say that her holiness is as yet of a consummate or definitive kind. A baptised baby is certainly regenerate, freshly innocent, holy in a sense that parallels the Church's initial holiness at her own birth from the side of Christ, or her own original manifestation at Pentecost in the Upper Room. Still, such an infant is not (yet) a great saint. From the start the Church was Holy Church, but her sharing in the holiness of her Lord is unending and only comes to full term in the final Kingdom.

The Church is catholic

What about the *catholicity* of the Church? We call her (with all due respect to the other Christian bodies which enjoy imperfect communion with her) 'the Catholic Church'. Roughly speaking, we could translate the word 'holistic' – bearing in mind that sometimes (especially in the Latin West) that has to do with the universality of her geographical outreach, and sometimes (especially in the Greek East) it concerns the completeness of her understanding of salvation and the needs of its recipient, man. St Cyril of Jerusalem in the lectures he gave to fourth-century catechumens in the church of the Anastasis (the Resurrection) gives five reasons why the Church can be called catholic:

- she extends to the ends of the earth
- she teaches all the doctrine needed for salvation
- she brings into her obedience every kind of human being
- she has the cure for every sort of sin
- she possesses in her members every form of virtue

So far as *quantitative* catholicity is concerned, we can sum this up by saying that the Church is a mediation of the plenary divine being, the result of the communication to her of the 'fullness' (St Paul's word in his Letter to the Colossians) of Christ her Head. The Swiss theologian-cardinal Hans Urs von Balthasar remarks that the Church's qualitative fullness is continually borrowed from the Saviour, but so borrowed as to be really her own. God's economics, evidently, are not identical with man's! In the divine Trinity, there is identity between God's oneness and the communicativeness of his being (his threefoldness) in an unsurpassable richness of life. In the Incarnation, the Word holds within himself the divine and human natures and with his human nature a microcosm of the world in all its dimensions – chemical, vegetative, sentient, rational. So it is not surprising that the Church his Body should be able to boast a huge variety of ministries and callings – from the patriarch of an ancient Oriental rite in Egypt or Syria, to an enclosed nun in a French Carmel, or a charity worker helping villagers in Africa's droughtlands to construct a simple dam. All these are for the building up of his body so that its members can grow in knowledge of the love of God which surpasses knowledge and 'be filled with all the fullness of God' (Eph 3:19). The miracle which the Spirit daily accomplishes in the Church is to foster communion without effacing (non-pernicious) differences, not only between different people but between different baptised cultures, or patterns of human living, or styles of thinking, or ways of praying, as expressed in the multiplicity of rites, spiritualities, theologies, Religious Orders, within the single Catholic Church. This is (when working properly) a coherent diversity typified by inner contrasts but not outright contradictions. Anarchy and cacophony have nothing to do with Christian liberty and the symphony of Catholic voices.

And then there is, as Cyril of Jerusalem would be quick to remind us, *quantitative* catholicity as well. The self-diffusive fullness of God expressed through Christ and the Spirit in the Church is not only intensive – to do with a quality of life under grace, it is also extensive, to do with the extension of that life to as many people as possible – and as many peoples, collectivities, as possible as well. Already in the Hebrew Bible the more universalist of the prophets took the goal of the divine plan to be the conversion of all the nations to the God of Israel. Newman in his *Essay on the Development of Christian Doctrine* found the fulfilment of this promise to be the coming of a *catholic* Church, a single society committed to worldwide outreach under divinely provided pastors. When St Luke describes Peter's Pentecost sermon as heard in their own languages by 'devout Jews from every nation under heaven (Acts 2:5), he obviously regards the apostles as getting their marching orders for spreading the faith throughout the known world. In his Apocalypse St John depicts an angel flying across the sky with

> an eternal Gospel to proclaim to those who live on the earth – to every nation and tribe and language and people (14:6).

And clearest of all there is the Great Commission at the end of St Matthew's Gospel, to 'go... and make disciples of all nations' (28:19), unmistakable words whose force no amount of fudge can destroy. If the Church is the bearer of the Gospel and its corporate embodiment, if she is therefore the sacrament of God's universally redemptive will in Christ, she must manifest an impulse – however politically incorrect – to be co-extensive with the race as such.

The Church is apostolic

That leaves us with the *apostolicity* of the Church. The Church exists by a movement of expansion from the original apostolic fellowship. That is why early Christian writers are so keen on showing the continuity of the churches with their apostolic founders, something attested in the drawing up of lists of bishops. The succession of apostolic ministers plays an important part in the continuing apostolicity of the Church. It should not be thought, however, that apostolicity is exclusively concerned with a relation to the past. The Twelve, the inner circle of the New Testament apostolate, also have an eschatological significance: they will sit on twelve thrones of judgement (Mt 19:28), just as in the Book of the Apocalypse their names are inscribed on the foundation stones of the heavenly Jerusalem (21:14). The covenant made by Jesus Christ, the Alpha and the Omega ('The Beginning and the End') and communicated via the apostles is a new and everlasting covenant which entails the gift of a share in final salvation, the ultimate good God has in store for man. So the beginning of the apostolic fellowship looks forward to its fulfilment – in history and beyond. The purpose of apostolicity is to unite the Church's beginning to her end, to assure the continuity of the saving revelation from the first hidden coming of Christ to his glorious second coming.

We cannot of course verify the claims of the Catholic Church to be the anticipation of the apostolic community of the End, for this by definition is beyond our gaze. But we can have better fortune where her claim to be the continuation of the apostolic community of the Beginnings is concerned, and that in three respects – apostolicity of origin; apostolicity of doctrine; apostolicity of ministerial succession. 'Your church goes back to Luther or Calvin, ours to the apostles' is how the argument from apostolicity runs. (Though the question, 'Where was your church before the Reformers?' sometimes elicited the counter-question, 'Where was your face this morning before you washed it?'!) Such apologetic concern with apostolicity of origin is extremely primitive, to be found, for example, in Clement of Rome, who may be writing before the end of the New Testament period itself – that is, before the final editing of the last book of the canon. St Thomas Aquinas links it to the Church's *firmitas*, her permanence or solidity, which for him derives from the fact that she teaches the same doctrine as the apostles themselves. Only a body originating from the apostles could know and indefectibly persevere in their teaching. In the controversies of the Reformation period, Catholics soon discovered that, important though the theme may be, it is easier to disprove the apostolicity of other communities than to prove that of one's own. At least we can say that any church which does not possess the doctrine of Christian antiquity cannot be the 'apostolic Church' of the Great Creed. That was an argument Protestants, and especially Anglicans, found they could use against Catholics, alleging that the latter had perhaps not subtracted from but anyway added to the faith of the early Church. Newman's theory of the 'development' of doctrine (homogeneously, self-consistently) was his attempt to defend precisely the apostolicity of the Catholic Church, and so of the 'apostolic succession' of its magisterial teachers.

The idea of the apostolic succession as a succession of hierarchs or ministers tends to be uppermost in the minds of most Catholics who have received a classical catechetical instruction and are conscious, however sketchily, of the historical background in disagreements with Anglicans, Lutherans and others. The continuity of such apostolic succession, as expressed in the consecration of bishops who are incorporated thereby into the apostolic college 'under and with Peter' (the Pope), has as its purpose the self-identity, and thus integrity, of Christian doctrine, and the assuring in the Church of a true sacramental worship. Men are initiated into this succession in order to secure the purity and fullness of the faith professed in baptism and the other sacraments, and so the confessional and liturgical structure of the Church as a whole. We are dealing here, as is seen archetypally in Jesus' commissioning of the Twelve after the Resurrection, with a mission of evangelisation and sacramental reconciliation with God. However – and here, so as to get things clear, we must be a little technical – while the succession of ministers is rendered apostolic *in point of material fact* by continuous transmission of the episcopate from the apostles through the laying on of hands, that succession is rendered apostolic *in point of formal principle* by the conservation of the doctrine transmitted by the apostles. Thus, for instance, the circumstance of the preservation of the apostolic succession by Dutch 'Old Catholics' or the Jacobite Church in Syria does not render these bodies identical with the 'apostolic Church' of the Creed. For the question has to be addressed, Do these bishops teach what the apostles explicitly or implicitly held the Gospel to be? Of course, it may not be possible in practice to determine what counts as apostolic doctrine until we have identified that Church which by the nature of the way it possesses the apostolic succession can be shown to be apostolic in origin. If I am asked to consider whether the doctrine of the Mother of God's exemption from original sin is apostolic, I may not be able to answer without noting how it was promulgated as dogma by the ministerial successor of Peter and received as true by the bishops in communion with him. That heuristic difficulty – a problem about finding something out – does not affect the basic fact that the pope and bishops are apostolic precisely by teaching the apostolic faith. The Church expands into the world by her apostolic mission as essentially an assembly of the *faithful*.

This essential link between apostolic doctrine and the apostolic ministry explains why no one can take on a ministerial function in the Church without making a profession of faith. No bishop-elect can be consecrated without such; no consecrated bishop can vote at an ecumenical Council without it. True, the teaching of the bishops acts as a rule, a measuring rod, for the faith of Catholic Christians, but their teaching is itself rule-grounded, conditioned by their fidelity to the apostolic Tradition, the Great Paradosis, as conserved by the Church and actualised in her through the guidance of the Holy

Spirit. That is why the faithful have not only the right but the duty to reject pastors who estrange themselves from the authentic succession by false teaching, teaching that fails to meet criteria of congruence with what is taught in the other local churches of the Catholic Church and notably in the church of Rome, 'in which', as St Irenaeus puts it, 'there has always been conserved that which is the Tradition from the apostles'. The Tradition, unimpaired and in its fullness, is the content of the succession.

Apostolicity of ministry – the apostolic succession – is an indispensable component of the apostolicity of the Church. It is as successors of the apostles that the bishops gather around them local constellations of the faithful – into patriarchates, dioceses, eparchies, vicariates apostolic, giving as they do so a share in their functions to priests and deacons for the service of such particular portions of the people of God. A few comments on aspects of the apostolic office often misunderstood may not be out of place here. They will be followed by an appeal to see the papacy and episcopate with the eschatological imagination, and not as boring bureaucrats (that, admittedly, is usually difficult with popes).

Though the bishops succeed to the ministry as equals of the apostles in the matter of pastoring their particular churches, they have, unlike the apostles, no charism of revelation. They are powerless to constitute a new normative tradition which is not an explication of the revelation of which the apostles are the final mediators and definitive witnesses. The 'charism of truth' as St Irenaeus calls it, enjoyed by the bishops 'according to the good pleasure of the Father' is, rather, a gift of teaching with certainty what the apostles explicitly or implicitly taught – a gift which, in the case of the Roman bishop alone, carries with it a personal charism of infallibility in such teaching. (By that very fact this is not, then, a capacity to add to the revelation the apostles were given.)

The only clear case of an apostolic minister succeeding

in a personal way to the pastoral office of an apostle concerns Peter (and Paul) at Rome. Otherwise, as the practice of ordaining bishops at the hands of multiple – classically three – consecrators indicates, bishops are said to succeed to the apostles corporately by enrolment in the *coetus*, the 'company', or *collegium*, the 'college' of the apostles – terms borrowed by the Second Vatican Council, with some earlier precedent, from Roman civil law. A grey area in Catholic 'ecclesiology' (thinking about the Church) is in what sense bishops in such apostolically founded sees as Antioch, Alexandria, Jerusalem and Constantinople can be regarded as in some kind of personal apostolic succession.

As I mentioned at the outset of these remarks on our *apostolic* Church, the consecration of bishops round the pope does not only continue sacramentally the original apostolic college around Peter. It also anticipates the city founded on the apostles of the Lamb in the Johannine Apocalypse. The liturgy sees the Twelve – and here we must learn to acquire its vision – continuously present to the Church through the ministry of the bishops. The bishops with the pope constitute a living icon of the Twelve around Peter. They do so not caught, as it were, frozen in inaction, but in their role of guarding the flock of God, above all by preserving it in the apostolic confession, for the salvation of the world. Calling the pope – even a bad pope – Peter *redivivus*, showing a bishop religious honour by, say, kissing his ring: this is not mere popular piety but an appropriate response of rhetoric and gesture to the sacramental figuration which pope and bishops offer to the heavenly apostles in the Church. It is to the Church as heaven on earth that I now turn.

Holy Persons, Holy Gifts

'*... the communion of saints...*'

His hands conjoined
super altare
his full chin crumpled
to the pectoral folds of
his newly washed focale
he begins the suffrage:
ORAMUS TE, DOMINE
pleading that the merits of
the Blessed departed
the veterani in the celestial castrum
& colonia 'in hevyn on hicht'
might assist him at the work
he is about to make

but in especial he asks the adjuvance of
these athletes of God
tokens of whom are cisted
immediately beneath
& central to
the Stone of Oblation
at which he now stands.

THE 'communion of the holy' in which we state our faith
in the Creed can be taken in either or both of two senses.
Since, as between masculine and neuter, the gender of the
genitive plural is indistinguishable in Latin (and the language of the Apostles' Creed, the Old Roman Creed, *is*
Latin), it may mean either a 'communion of holy persons'
or 'a communion of holy things, or gifts' – or conceivably,

and this will be the view taken here, it may mean both of these together. In the Greek East, the corresponding formula was used not in the Creed but for sacramental purposes, and would be taken to mean, then, communion in the Church's mysteries, and above all the Holy Eucharist. West of Ravenna, the theologians of Charlemagne's empire were aware of this and influenced by it. From the early Middle Ages onwards the Latin Catholic divines seek to integrate this 'Oriental' meaning into their commentaries on the Creed. But the Western interpretation of *communio sanctorum* was always predominantly personalist – it meant the martyrs, and the saints in a more restricted sense of that word, but then eventually all believers who are called, at least, to be saints, and indeed the patriarchs and prophets of the Old Testament and even the holy angels. The last named categories apart, it is easy to see why the Church has refused to decide between these two possibilities. How could the holiness of the Church's members be separated from that divine holiness which is mediated by the sacraments of the Church?

Holy persons

'Holy persons' exist for the Church in her own three states: on pilgrimage, undergoing purification, and in Glory. In the holy warfare of the Church militant it is possible, thank God, to meet with living saints. Saving the Church's judgement, Mother Teresa of Calcutta, whom the author met whilst an undergraduate at the Old Palace in Oxford in the late 1960s, would seem to be such – the sweet Christ's charity in womanly form on earth. The evangelical impression she made will doubtless be more effective than any organisational initiative, not to speak of any book. But the continuing history of salvation is being written by actors in heaven – in the Church of glory – as well as by actors on earth. The uniqueness of Christ's mediation of salvation is shown in the way he enables the saints in heaven to co-operate in its extension by participating in his fullness as the only Redeemer of the human race. From the Church's heavenly members, those who are most closely bonded to him, there flows what the Second Vatican Council calls (thinking in the first place of the Blessed Virgin) *influxus salutaris*, 'saving in-pouring', a stream of refreshing water, upon their earthly brethren who are still on pilgrimage, often thirsty. It is a major motif in the lives – and especially the deaths – of the saints. St Dominic promised that he would be more useful after death to his brethren than he had been in life, and the antiphon sung in his honour, *Pie pater Dominice,* reminds him of that undertaking. St Thérèse of the Child Jesus declared she would 'shower down roses', 'spend her heaven doing good on earth'. We can suppose that this takes place in a special way at the liturgy, for the same worship we perform beneath the veils of sacramental signs they celebrate in unveiled reality before the Face of God. (That is the point of the citation from David Jones', 'The Kensington Mass' at the head of this chapter.) From this conjunction of two agencies arises the opportunity for those who have already attained perfection to communicate spiritual good things to their comrades on earth. In a holy exchange, their intercession brings gifts to us, as we give our veneration to them. Praying to the saints is a vital aspect of Catholic devotional life.

In *The Way of Perfection*, Teresa of Avila pre-empts an obvious objection. We shall immediately be told (classically, by Protestants) that speaking with the friends of God is unnecessary. It is enough to have God himself. But, she replies, a great means of having God *is* to speak with his friends. The immediate presence of the triune God to us does not *obliterate* mediations of the divine presence, it *fosters* them as never before. It is because the God of grace is so that dialogue with the saints, communion with the saints, studying the lives of the saints as a source both for understanding revelation and reforming our own lives, is integral to the Catholic way. After all, the very existence

109

of the Church and her tradition, sacraments and institutions has as its rationale the production of saints. The personal holiness of the Church's members is what the Catholic thing is all about. (At the same time, it is also true that no Catholic saint would be such without the Catholic Church – and that is no sociological platitude but a truth of faith.)

The absorbing interest of the study of the saints is that, while none lives a life without lessons for others (who may differ from him or her as chalk from cheese), their missions are so unlike. Our particular mission is the form of sanctity predestined for us, it is the way God wants us to dispose ourselves to his plan. Our temperament, the slant of our human nature, our particular set of aptitudes and inclinations will of course be relevant to this, and yet our mission – our path to holiness – cannot simply be 'read off' from these natural predispositions and gifts. Assessing our nature does not by itself lead to a just idea of God's gracious intention for us, for this requires discernment of God's will through meditation, prayer, the calls on us of others and the providential leading of events. The liturgy has its own categories of holiness: martyrs and apostles, pastors and virgins, and others. But looking at the matter as panoramically as possible we can say the missions of the saints fall under two principal classifications (here I follow Balthasar again): 'customary' and 'representative' sanctity. *Customary* holiness flows from the fulfilling of vocation by way of the normal, unspectacular daily round of the Church's common life. *Representative* holiness entails God's singling out of individuals for some unusual mission in the Church – which, however, as with the founders of the great Religious Orders, may well act as a catalyst for others to follow in their steps. The representative saints suggest new types of holiness in the Church, whereas the customary saints live out a holiness of which any well instructed Christian is conscious – though not every such Christian lives in the sacrificial fashion that would let him or her become a 'customary saint'. *Personal* mission is always deployed as a unique variant of either customary or representative holiness. Many of the saints embody intenser forms of the 'ordinary' Christian virtues, faith, hope, charity and the evangelically transmuted 'cardinal' virtues known to the pagan ancients: justice, fortitude, temperance, prudence. They come as no surprise to us. They are simply singularly pure and fruitful expressions of the common life of the Church, shining examples of our own kind: thus, for example, St Margaret of Scotland for the laity, St Hugh of Lincoln for the clergy. But there are other saints – and these are frequently the ones who attract most devotion from Catholics – who are altogether out of the ordinary, their way of life hardly imitable by people with (perfectly legitimate) ordinary preoccupations and concerns. Figures like St Francis of Assisi, St Anthony of Padua, St Thérèse of Lisieux, are not in any obvious way role-models. But the devotion of the faithful instinctively recognises them as vast globes of light, fireplaces of warmth, placed in the Church by God as living expressions of the everlasting Gospel, in its full dimensions. To understand the Word of God, it is desirable to have some entry into the world of just such saints.

But what of those other 'holy persons' of the Church, the 'Holy Souls' undergoing purification, the Church in Purgatory? The instinct of the faithful includes a certitude that we can come to the aid of the departed by our intercession. The Church began quite spontaneously to pray for her dead members as well as her living ones. The first signs of it are popular inscriptions scratched on the walls of the catacombs and suchlike places where the early Christians buried their dead. 'Give peace to Marius'; 'peace to you, Cecilia'. Nobody had theories about it; it was the instinctive reaction of Christian faith. Christ, the Lord of the Church, had risen from the dead, and in the radiant light of the first Easter morning in a garden, the first disciples could see life in relation to this man who not only was alive but had shown himself to be the Lord of life, and the Lord *for* life, the one who revealed his re-creating power by a life stronger than death. And if re-creating, then creating! Biological life is possible because it is the gift of Christ, through whom all things were made. If the Source of life, both old and new, is Christ, then the decisive thing is to be near that Source. Biology, the science of life, becomes Christology, the science of Christ. Biological rupture does not sunder the communion of charity. And this includes the forgotten dead, the 'poor souls' who have no one to pray for them. Such solidarity with the dead enlarges our horizons; it brings home to us that our philanthropy is not to be restricted to material things; it strengthens our awareness of indebtedess to the past, the ancestors, and discourages any temptation we may feel to spiritualist or occultist aberrations.

Holy gifts

The sacred liturgy is the conversation of the Church with her Spouse, Jesus Christ. Its outward forms are not always lovely. Not all priests, religious or lay people responsible for the celebration of the liturgy have a sensibility fine tuned to its treasures, and the rites promulgated by Church authority sometimes show – quite apart from issues of inadequate translation – humanity's perverse gift of supplanting things of great value with things of less. Still, the liturgy, because it is the exchange of love between Christ and the Church, is all glorious within.

The celebration of the sacraments, and notably the Mass, is the high point of Catholic worship. All the sacraments take their vigour from the Passion of Christ. The lance thrust that wounded his side was the trauma from which there originated the grace of these signs that sustain the Church's life. The signs themselves range further than that – though the heart of the Mass *is* the sacramental translation of the Death on the Tree. We saw in chapter 5, 'Ultimate sacrifice', how the Paschal Mystery – running from Good

Friday through Easter to Pentecost – is essentially a mystery of saving worship where the Son sums up the mission expressed in his Incarnation and public ministry by a supreme act of praise of the Father which is also his efficacious pleading with the Father for the redemption of the world. That offering, accepted by the Father when he raised Christ from the dead and exalted him to his right hand, was made savingly effective for others when the glorified Lord became at Pentecost co-principle with the Father of the Holy Spirit in *his* mission to the world. Because the Paschal Mystery is a mystery of saving worship it can also be the source whence issues the sacramental life of the Church. The sacraments are precisely acts of praise and pleading, carried out on this divinely given basis. The missions of the Son and Spirit make it possible for the same saving worship our Head offered in his Death and Resurrection to have its scope extended to us, his members. Indeed, in the words of St Leo the Great, 'all that is visible in the life of our Redeemer has passed into his mysteries', the sacraments of the Church. With the Ascension, Christ passed out of sight beyond this world's visible horizon. But this is not because God has gone back on the incarnational principle, his desire to meet us through bodily, sensuous signs. The only reason why Christ is now invisible to the world is that the world (including ourselves) is not yet ready for him, not as he now is, in Glory. From heaven he prepares us, via the regime of the Holy Spirit, for a sight of him face to face in the bodily encounter of the Parousia. The sacraments make possible a continuing tryst or meeting between Christ and sinful humanity. They function by rendering the mysteries of Christ's life – and above all the mystery of his life-giving Death – newly actual (that is, present and active, here and now) in such a way as to inaugurate final salvation on earth.

The sacraments look like – and indeed anthropologically they are – miniature ritual dramas. The sacramental actions mimic various aspects of the saving acts of God in Christ:

they are their symbolic representations. But not only that. The risen Christ by his divine power re-actualises the redemptive acts he carried out in his humanity for our salvation and makes the sacraments their prolongation in our space, our time. I too can be at Calvary, in the Garden, the Upper Room – and indeed by the Jordan, or at Cana in Galilee where the God-man graced the state of marriage by his blessing. But just as to have been there myself, in the first century of the Christian era, but as a casual observer, only, would have availed me nothing, so here too I am to be present not merely by material reception of the sacraments but as a seeker after grace.

And what *is* the grace – the participation in divine life, but in a human way – the sacraments give? It is sanctifying grace, but such grace given according to that purpose which the sacramental sign – the particular symbolic structure of any one sacrament – suggests. For each sacrament has its own rationale, its own place in Christian living and the divine scheme. To that extent, we need to look at the seven sacraments in the distinctiveness of each. Meanwhile, we can note that in every case it will be, in one way or another, a matter of God-given influences on human character working themselves out through a life of discipleship through the means the Saviour has appointed for the building up of saints.

• *Baptism*, a ritual sprinkling with water, is the sacramental counterpart of the natural generation and birth – in the waters of parturition – which give us our earthly life. In baptism, we are re-born supernaturally to the higher life of grace. To be born is already a marvel. Without lifting a finger, the *neonatus* has become a shareholder in the commonwealth of creation. The earth, sky, sea, the animals, birds and plants are his fellow-creatures; his parents and all who wish him well are his brothers and sisters. The holy angels are his guardians. Unfortunately, this wonderful world is also a wicked place, the home of violence and hate; envy, bitterness, resentment; betrayal, ingratitude, indifference. No rite of the Church, even one of which Christ is the primary agent, can exempt a child from the effect of these realities, or an adult from their continuance. What baptism *can* do, however, is to liberate someone from the drive to collaborate with evil, to take forward its reign. It can ensure that the neophyte does nothing damnably awful. By healing the wound in our nature – the complicity with corruption second nature to us as members of a fallen race – the Holy Spirit provides us in this sacrament with a new ground for our acting, a new principle for not only our decisions but our impulses as well. The power infused into the soul in baptismal regeneration is the power of charity, the sacrificial love shown by Christ. The Creator stooped down to enter this world as its Redeemer not only by restoring our nature – marvellous though that is – but also to raise up our personalities so that we might share – knowingly and willingly – his own divine life. Incorporation into the Church tells us that we are not just to be simply human creatures, even good ones. We are to be companions in the society of the Holy Trinity, enjoying together the vision of God.

• *Confirmation* fortifies, develops and perfects the supernatural life communicated to us in baptism – just as man is meant by natural growth to reach physical and moral maturity. That 'maturity' (the idea must not be overdone; there is a sense in which the greatest graces are childlike) carries responsibilities. Baptism, in signifying our entry into the new and everlasting covenant sets up a relationship with all those who are to form part of this covenant. It points towards an ecclesial mission – a task we are to be given vis-à-vis other people. Confirmation, the laying on of hands with anointing, commissions us for this task and gives us the sacramental grace to perform it. As with the apostles in their receiving the Pentecostal Spirit on the first Whit Sunday, Confirmation confers a mission of witness and the help needed to accomplish it. It is full entry into the order of the laity, more magnificent than any order of chivalry, since this is the royal and universal priesthood of the faithful. To be incorporated into the Messianic covenant is wonderful: a lifetime does not suffice to absorb it. Yet there is a *quid pro quo*. One must agree to be confirmed, to be mandated for the Messianic mission. Every Catholic is obliged to be – quietly or noisily, by word or deed – an *apostolic* Christian.

• *The Holy Eucharist*, the all-holy bread and wine of the sacrament of the altar, gives the children of God a heavenly nourishment to feed their spiritual life, just as physical life and strength draw continued sustenance from food and drink. They feed on Christ the living Bread and drink from the fruit of the True Vine, the Blood which issued from the wound in his side. The kind of meal the Mass is derives from its character as *the Christian sacrifice,* that is, the Sacrifice of Christ now co-offered by the Church. The divine life was outpoured on Calvary where each Trinitarian Person contributed to that act of reconciliation re-uniting the world to God – the Father willing and receiving the Sacrifice, the Son executing it, the Spirit communicating its effects. So the Mass, as Calvary's sacramental expression, is better able to unite human beings to God and to each other in God, than anything else we know. It is not, notice, the sacrament of just any old kind of bonding – *camaraderie*, for example, or the unity of the cultural, ethnic or social category to which the people celebrating it may belong. The Eucharist is exclusively the sacrament of *paschal charity.* It flows from the total gift of God to the world in the life-giving death of the Son and the spiritual love it generates can only be the sort which gives itself to God and all human beings without distinction. There is nothing tribal about the Mass. It is universal petition just as it is universal praise.

And universal praise it certainly is, as the whole cosmos

116

and humanity with it is summoned to be present – the angels, human voices and material elements. In the Eucharist the heavenly and the earthly are brought into communion as one – which makes this the perfect sacrament of the Kingdom, itself the fusion, precisely, of earth with heaven. This communion comes about through incorporation into Christ by feeding at the Eucharistic feast where he is 'substantially' present thanks to the conversion of the being of bread and wine into his own sacred body and precious Blood. Christ mediates the divine Love by using created matter, gathering the faithful to him from within their own incarnate condition. The body of the Lord is the launching pad from which humanity is lifted beyond itself to the threshold of the Age to Come with all its powers. Joined to Christ, who in his risen Glory is the centre of heaven, the faithful cross the boundary between this-worldly time and the definitive future, the new Jerusalem – as the Byzantine liturgy with its radiant other-worldly beauty is peculiarly well placed to show.

But Catholics do not only venerate the Holy Eucharist in the course of its celebration. They return to it in between times in adoration and thanksgiving for this unique bodily mode of his presence to his people as their strength and stay. They do so either through personal prayer before the Eucharistic Tabernacle (prominently displayed in Western Catholic churches this is a small shrine housing the vessels that contain the consecrated Elements), or by taking part in the corporate veneration of the Eucharistic Bread, God-with-us, most frequently in the rite called Benediction of the Blessed Sacrament. In Patrick Kavanagh's *Lough Derg*, which conjures up the austerities and consolations of a mixed bag of the faithful at a Donegal pilgrimage site,

The rosary is said and Benediction.
The Sacramental sun turns round and 'Holy, Holy,
    Holy'
The pilgrims cry, striking their breasts in Purgatory.

The exposition of the sacred Host shows the supernatural Sun of Righteousness, Jesus Christ, to the eyes of the Church's contemplation and love.

• *Penance* is the sacrament that cures any moral wounds of the soul sustained after baptism, restoring it to the life of grace, after a fashion comparable to medical remedy for illness. This *sacrament of penance* presupposes a *virtue of penitence*. Unless I am contrite for my sins, and know compunction – the awareness that, unless the grace of God assist, moral disaster can at any time befall me and my neighbour, I do not approach this tribunal of mercy in a fit spirit. 'Why do you need to confess your sins to a priest?' ask many Christians from the Reformation churches. In breathing the Holy Spirit on the apostles and telling them, 'If you forgive the sins of any, they are forgiven' (Jn 20:23), we do not think the Saviour made a mental reservation, excluding the post-baptismal sins of Christians. Besides, the act of confessing increases humility, and strengthens the conscience, while the act of absolution pronounced by the Church's minister confers a grace our moral life can use. Still, people use this sacrament differently. In the strict letter of the canons, it is necessary only for 'mortal' sins, those whoppers (in the classical discussion by the Fathers, apostasy, murder, adultery) which destroy the grace-life within us. But there are many other occasions when recourse to the sacrament is appropriate – for some turning-point in life; at the approach of the great feasts of the Church; if there is a new task ahead or a sense of guilty failure over an old one; if there is some particular difficulty to be worked at. And indeed, the sacrament always makes sense as a receptive gesture expressive of our dependence on the mercy of God.

• *The Anointing of the Sick*, a rite where olive oil, mixed with chrism, is applied to the body, is the sacrament which obliterates the remaining trace-effects or lingering consequences of spiritual sickness by giving the soul – in the context of physical suffering and ultimately of dying – new graces that fortify it for the future. It might be compared to good nursing, combined with rest. Anointing maintains and strengthens communion with God and my neighbour at times when that unity is compromised by the debilitating effects of sickness and old age. The tendency of the sick body to become an alien object to the mind is corrected by the grace of Christ's Spirit. The tendency of suffering to make me exclusively attentive to myself and to dislocate my relations with others is rectified by that Spirit. The anguish of illness, prompted by the experience of finitude and mortality, is also healed as the sacrament enables me to accept the fact that I shall, eventually, die and to accept that fact in a manner both creative and sacrificial, which makes of death a way to God. The sacrament, then, does not always result in physical healing – clearly: if things were so unsubtle I should not have to write this 'invitation to share the faith of the Catholic Church', there would be a stampede to get in! But that does not mean the Anointing of the Sick, when given as the Last Anointing – 'Extreme Unction' – has failed in its purpose. All the sacraments are sacraments of hope, as well as faith and love. They look forward to the Age to Come, and allow us to take hold of it.

• *Order* is the sacrament whereby the Church, the super-natural society, is furnished with ordained ministers just as natural society – not secular society, which is unnatural, but a healthy pagan society – needs those who are not only leaders and teachers but also celebrants of cult. In the case of the Church such ministers act by virtue of the commission given by Christ to the holy apostles to whose company they are aggregated by the laying on of hands with prayer. The apostolic Tradition comes down to us in the form of the apostolic succession. Catholics are not over-impressed by the argument that a 'tactile' succession of ministers, forming a living *chain* through history by the laying on of

119

first apostolic and then episcopal hands is a kind of materialism. It is a sacrament, and therefore *naturally* an example of Christian materialism, cohering with the character of the Incarnation itself. The Word incarnate willed that his apostles should at need incorporate others into their mission and so entrust to them the tradition of his teaching and the Gospel signs that are the sacraments of the Kingdom, and do so by a gesture of commissioning until his return in Glory. There are three grades or steps ('orders') in this sacrament; the deacon, the presbyter, and the bishop. All three have liturgical, teaching and pastoral or at least (in the case of the deacon) charitable roles. They are conveniently distinguished in a little formula: the deacon has responsibility for the Word; the presbyter for the Word and the Eucharist; the bishop for the Word, the Eucharist and the Church. As is shown by their offering the Eucharistic Sacrifice, both presbyter and bishop are minis-terial priests who act in the 'person' – the name and role – of Christ himself as Head of his Church, as well as doing so in the 'person' of the Church herself. They act, then, for the 'whole Christ', Head and members, and this high privilege as well as burden means that their lives are not their own. They are expropriated into the service of God and of the 'common' or universal priesthood of the faithful. This makes their priesthood not only functional but also iconic – one reason why it is reserved to those who exercise it in the same male gender that Christ himself inhabits. The sacred vestments of the liturgy are a good expression of anonymity for the sake of the High Priesthood of Christ.

• *Marriage* is the sacrament which allows new members of the Church to be engendered within her, just as natural society needs propagating as well. The sacramental 'layer' is the deepest stratum a Catholic excavator would find in marriage, which implies, then, it is not the only one. In the first place, marriage is a natural institution necessary for society's flourishing. In entering it people take on a publicly defined way of life, with an already existing set of duties and responsibilities. They have to use their imaginations to occupy this institution creatively, but they do not create it out of their imaginations. Because marriage is a public institution also for the Church (and not just for the State), it is fitting for her to lay down canons about entering marriage, living in it and sometimes, unfortunately, leaving it. But then secondly, as such an institution, marriage must have its goals – and the Church sees the pursuit of these, when carried out by Christians in the spirit of discipleship, as a form of ministry or mission. In entering marriage, a person takes on a threefold ministry: to the person he or she marries by way of love and fidelity, helping the other to grow in the life of nature and of grace; to the children they will have or may have, building up an environment in which they can blossom naturally and supernaturally; to the rest of mankind – in so far as my family circle can be what the French call *un foyer chrétien*, 'a Christian home', drawing others into its own warmth. Meaning: other families, newcomers, visitors, the handicapped, the lonely. This is already to go deeper than the institutional, but it is not yet to reach the ultimate bedrock (no pun intended!) of the sacrament. By accepting a lifelong sacrificial commitment one to another, the married couple enter into the endless mystery of the redemptive love of God which reached its supreme expression on the Cross of Christ. They become, without always being aware of it, a mediation of the fruitful suffering of Christ just as Christ is a mediation of the ultimate holy mystery, that uncreated self-giving we call the blessed Trinity. In marriage, erotic love and friendship are integrated into redemptive love, and become the materials of that love. The sign that this integration has actually taken place in their lives lies in their readiness to forgive the hurts which extreme closeness to others always brings, a readiness to be reconciled and start afresh. In the era of grace, divorce should be superfluous.

The 'holy persons' and 'holy gifts' that are the primary referents of the phrase *communio sanctorum* in the Creed have prompted a wider context of sacrality in the worshipping and devotional life of Catholics. Among the most important expressions of this are: relics; images; and music, all of which find house and home in the liturgy of the Church.

Sacred relics

Relics assist the Scriptures and the sacraments to do their work, by insinuating how access is still available to the holy persons whose relics they are, despite the seeming barriers of space and time. St Polycarp of Smyrna appears to have been a direct disciple of the Apostle John. He was martyred around 155 and the event was written up shortly afterwards, evidently by an eye-witness. After his burning by the pro-consul of Asia, the faithful gathered up his remains for suitable housing against the day of their liturgical veneration.

> Thus we, at last, took up his bones, more precious than precious stones, and finer than gold, and put them where it was meet. There the Lord will permit us to come together according to our power in gladness and joy, and celebrate the birthday of his martyrdom, both in memory of those who have already contested, and for the practice and training of those whose fate it shall be.

Here we have in germ the theology of the cult of relics as that can be found in the writings of the great Fathers of East and West: St Basil and St John Chrysostom, St Ambrose and St Augustine. The excellence of the martyrs renders their bodily remains precious; their relics are a reminder that their lives and death should be a model for all. There is also the little matter of the evidence for divine working through relics. The historian will be on the watch for legendary accretions here. Yet there is congruence with Christian claims for the Resurrection of Christ if the glorious resurrection of all the faithful is anticipated after a fashion in the mediation of his grace through the earthly remains of his saints.

Holy images

Icons – a term I use here as synonymous with holy images – have proved more eloquent as representations of the saving Cross or of the saints than have relics themselves, which is why very frequently the image is called, in the decoration of reliquaries, to the relic's aid. Since the life of God the Son on earth was a human life in every sense (sin alone excepted), it was necessarily a life capable of depiction in artistic terms. As soon as the Church ceased to be a persecuted sect and became a tolerated religion in the Roman empire a Christian art began openly to flourish. The fact of the Incarnation made it inevitable. That God had revealed himself in a definitive way through the human nature assumed by the Son meant that henceforth true belief about the divine could be expressed by works of art. St John of Damascus wrote in defence of the making and venerating of the icons:

> Now that God has appeared in the flesh and lived among men I make an image of the God who can be seen. I do not venerate matter, but I venerate the Creator of matter, who for my sake became material and deigned to dwell in matter, who through matter effected my salvation.

Although there were hesitations among some early Christian teachers, who remembered the injunctions of the Old Testament about the danger of idolatry, anonymous artists, moved by the sense of the faithful, were soon producing a whole gallery of images of Christ, his Mother and his saints, as well as symbols denoting the great events of

Christ's life, and the Church and sacraments which pass on their saving power. In the simple frescoes of the Roman catacombs; the more complex narrative scenes, usually in mosaic, of the great Basilican churches; and the portraits which might be found simply in private homes, the Christians of the first centuries put into line and colour the divine redemption of which they were so conscious. In 787, at the Seventh Ecumenical Council, the Church defined the legitimacy of holy images. In the same place where over four centuries earlier, in 325, she had proclaimed it as of faith that the Son is 'one in being with the Father', she now solemnly taught that the icons were (as we might put it) 'one in meaning' with the same Son, and the revelation of the Father which, through the work of the Holy Spirit, he brought into the world.

Sacred music

The Church has her own patrimony of music, first and foremost in the case of the Roman liturgy, Gregorian chant – but the Eastern liturgies all have some analogue of Western plainchant, an ancient, pure monodic music with a hieratic character, a consecrated music whose origins are lost in time immemorial. Alongside the chant we find a more 'developed' sacred music, generally polyphonic in character, as well as a popular repertoire, often of dubious value. It is the first of these which is *the* music *par excellence* of the Church. It is a music where sound is redeemed, where the sensuous becomes not only the servant of spirit but the vehicle of grace. Like Christ the chant is *poor, chaste,* and *obedient.* Its poverty of means (no instrumental accompaniment, polyphony or harmony) becomes, at the hands of its anonymous makers, a way to spiritual freedom, as Christ's adoption of poverty made him freer in the service of his Father. The chant's chastity in avoiding sensuality and sentiment enables it to become light and flexible, with the exquisite spontaneity theological tradition has ascribed to the resurrected flesh. And the chant is obedient in accepting the role of a servant in regard to the sacred liturgy, just as the Word made flesh accepted the part of a servant for the world's salvation. It is a music which pacifies and purifies sensibility and tends to recollection. Via the texts of Scripture, it may give expression to love and hatred, desire and hope, confidence and boldness, weariness or terror, and yet everything that is passionate, and perhaps anarchically so, in these moods is overmastered by the immensity of the divine peace. It was with a true evangelical instinct that the Roman see – at the time when, in the nineteenth century, the 'Caecilian' movement (originating in Bavaria), having rediscovered Palestrina, was trying to re-introduce Renaissance polyphony into the liturgy, at the expense of the then alternatives – operatic-style settings, the sentimental chromatic harmonies of Romanticism or the simple ver-nacular hymns preferred by liturgical puritans, gave its support to none of these but rather to the revival of the chant. Happy the parishioner who finds a primer of plain-song in his pew, and a small schola for the more difficult pieces in his parish church, or at least a music in use that emulates in the vernacular some at any rate of the chant's qualities.

Both sacraments and these select examples of a wider sacrality have their proper home in the *liturgical year*. Catholics live in liturgical time. The liturgy teaches how to make divine salvation our own by presenting to us the mysteries – the events – in which that salvation was won for us and given to us as Christ lived on earth, died for our sake and was exalted to the Father's right hand, there to mediate all our relations with God until he comes again in Glory. The liturgical year, in the West from Advent to the Sunday called 'Christ the King', represents the whole course the Word followed as he came forth from the Father so as to scoop us up and return to the Father, now accompanied by his disciples. It is a *cycle*, then, just as the Church's year is a cycle, and in this cycle time is united with eternity. In the original cycle – the life of Christ from Incarnation to Ascension – the work of our redemption was essentially accomplished. But the Lord wanted it to be so accomplished that we could participate in it, really share it, and he gave us the chance of that participation through the Church he founded. He continues to make available to us in the liturgy the same saving deeds by which he healed and raised up human nature to share the Father's life. That is why the Second Vatican Council calls the sacred liturgy the 'summit toward which the activity of the Church is directed; ... the fountain from which all her power flows' (*Sacrosanctum Concilium, 10*). In the different seasons of the year and on the great festivals, the Lord unfolds for us the various aspects of the salvation he achieved and invites us to respond appropriately. So each season and feast has its own grace to offer, in a fashion which taken cumulatively presents to us the whole work of Christ for our sanctification, our union with God.

Antidote to Evil

'... the forgiveness of sins'

Shall I confess my sins? Then help me tell:
In lust I scorch, and drown in riot, pine
With envy, and with looseness moulder, shine
In easy fortunes, and I in harder quell.
I shrink with baseness, and with pride I swell.
Fear makes me stoop, detraction repine,
With avarice I twist, and do untwine
With largess, heaven I buy with wish, but sell
My soul for pleasure, with ambition
I overreach, with shame I sneak, dissention
Doth rend asunder, kindness not content me,
Repose doth slow my mind, and study break,
Knowledge doth cloy, and ignorance torment me.
Shall I confess my sins? Then help me speak.

Unhealthy outlook

THERE certainly seems to be a need for such an 'antidote',
not least in such advanced Western societies as our own.
Not all vices bear a public face. I do not wish to make my
readers flesh creep. Still, the vices newspapers report and
social statisticians chart – especially if the vigour of those
vices is increasing – can make the point most tellingly.
They also add a certain urgency to that appeal for the
'conversion of England' I made in my Introduction.

It is often argued... [writes an analyst for the *Centre
for Policy Studies*] that there is 'no new thing under

the sun', as Ecclesiastes puts it. But where, until now, has there been anything like the observation [in the *Guardian* by a spokesman for Castle Morpeth Council] that residents of private care homes are 'income-producing raw material' and, when dead, represent 'the waste produced by the business'?

Is it a new moral thing, or an old, that a lesbian couple practising 'self-insemination' should, before breaking up their partnership, have had 'two "DIY" babies, using a pickle-jar and a syringe?' or that another similar couple should purchase... the frozen sperm of a stranger via the Internet?...

And when, until now, would a distinguished surgeon, describing 'the prospect of taking a dead person's face and draping it over the skull of a living man or woman'... declare, that 'it is simply like changing the cloth of an armchair'? (*The Times*, 23/9/97)...

Is it an old moral thing, or a new moral thing, that there is now 'an arson attack in at least three schools every day'?... Or that one in three churches can expect to be the target of an attack of some kind – theft, vandalism, arson – each year?... Or that malicious vandalism is now the biggest cause of railway accidents?... Or that eighty-six percent of alarm calls in the Metropolitan Police area are shown to be false?... Or that trees, shrubs and bushes planted in memory of the Dunblane victims were stolen within days from the local cemetery?...

Has there ever before been such violence directed in a time of peace by youth... against the frailest and most elderly, so that even women in their eighties come to be savaged and raped?... Is it an old thing under the sun, or a new, that doctors – it is estimated that *one thousand* of them are assaulted each year – teachers, and priests should feel themselves at such risk from those for whom they care? When, before,

could nursing be regarded as Britain's 'most danger-
ous profession', with one nurse in three, compared
with one policemen in four, suffering an act of
violence... in accident and emergency units?...

This selection of pretty horrors does not mean that our
society is uniquely corrupt. It does mean that social
ameliorism is false. It is not the case that, thanks to secular
benevolence – on the part of the State, professional
organisations, or others – everything is getting better and
better every day in every way.

The first words of the Saviour in his public ministry
were, 'Be penitent!' I prefer this as a translation to 'Repent!'
because the English phrase (as distinct from single word)
is less likely to be misunderstood as simply a 'one-off'
occurrence. Penitence is an abiding dimension of the
Christian life.

The all-sufficient Sacrifice of Christ furnishes, as we
make it our own by penitent faith, the ground of our
forgiveness. From it flow fresh ethical resources for us.
The indwelling of the Pentecostal Spirit flowers in the life
of the virtues, which can be made as easy as breathing by
the Gifts of the Holy Spirit. This is a new moral life that
is altogether a gift of grace, one way of sharing in the
Resurrection life of Christ by the Holy Spirit. And
irrespective of grand schemes of social improvement, it
has endless repercussive consequences for the social world.

And yet, even for those in receipt of the Pentecostal
grace of the atoning work of the Incarnate, sin goes on
happening. Even if there have been saints who seem to
have danced their way into heaven, they will certainly
have known temptation, which is the very stuff of holy
warfare.

Dealing with evil

In treating of holy warfare, the ascetical tradition of the Church speaks plain: it is not enough to deal with human malfeasance. This war begins in heaven. The evil angels, though no longer much preached about in the churches of the North Atlantic civilisation, have not ceased to harass man. What they have done, as ever in human history, is to change their masks, or, to put it more philosophically, the schemata of their self-presentation. They have presented themselves in different ways in different periods. They can be pagan gods who lead human beings astray, to immorality. Or demons experienced as inhabiting people, like the aliens in John Wyndham's novel *The Midwich Cuckoos*. Or again, the evil angels can manifest themselves in totalitarian visions of politics, or in pansexual pictures of happiness. Or they can come over as neuroses that sap our energy, our ability to practise charity towards God, our neighbour and ourselves. Theirs is a causality of transcendental influence – so this is not to be taken as an *alternative* to other, more empirical explanations. What they have in common is that, wherever they appear, they disfigure the image of man: his dignity, his nobility. Through the Fall of these angels, their wills no longer attain the Supreme Good for which they were made. And so they use their superabundant angelic energy to disrupt and distort the existence of lesser spiritual beings whom God in his goodness would draw to himself. That is why the decisive victory over the evil powers was not Jesus' exorcisms but his death and Resurrection which took our humanity in a definitive way into the life of God.

But though we have had 'D' Day – the crucial engagement, we have not had 'V' Day, the cessation of hostilities. And meanwhile the spiritual desperation of the Archfiend makes him pursue any number of strategies – in one age to insinuate gross exaggerations of the power he is permitted; in another to encourage incredulity about his very existence. The one trait these strategies share is lovelessness, for the essence of Satan is that he is a spiritual creature without love.

The Fall renders us his miniatures, not in lovelessness alone but in deviousness too. The forgiveness of sins is a principal objective of the divine economy. It involves: communicating to us our need of forgiveness (and thus the registering of sin); and providing us with the means of effective forgiveness (for the overcoming of sin). It is little use having the insight to grasp our condition unless we also have the power to change our behaviour. To enable us to measure our ethical shortfall, the Church teaches morals; to enable us to do something about that falling short, she gives us access to new ethical resources.

That is a poor monetary image suggested by the phrase 'the "divine" economy'. Dante knew better what it is about when he called it *la vita nuova*, 'the new life'. That life begins with personal conversion in baptismal waters, but continues in the exposure of the neophyte to the healing and life-giving Word of God and the other sacraments of the Church, assisted by all the helps of devotion and discipline which her spiritual treasury commands. Thanks to the indwelling of the Holy Spirit, the moral life of Christians can flower in the virtues, whose practice is made easier by the Spirit's gifts. We shall not grow until we make those virtues altogether our own. As St Teresa remarks in *The Interior Castle*, if we do not strive for the virtues and practise them we shall always be dwarfs.

Teaching moral truth

Perhaps the most perennial heresy in the Devil's intellectual wardrobe is the denial – so convenient – of the objectivity of truth, goodness and beauty. If Satan's name, according to the Gospels, is 'legion', then radical pluralism is his favoured doctrine. The 'modern mind' and a fortiori the 'post-modern mind' rule out any possibility of knowing revealed truth, a truth originating from beyond human intelligence as a gift. But unfortunately the kinds of truth such mind-sets do recognise are somewhat unreliable. The objective truth achieved by scientific method is regarded by the practitioners of that method as probabilistic in character. The subjective truth of aesthetic and ethical preference is, by definition, not liable to conclusive debate. This places the Catholic Church in a counter-cultural position, for she claims that human reason can reach certainty on such matters as the existence of God and the principles of the natural moral law. The revelation which brought her into existence has steadied her grasp of the founding axioms of moral reasoning. G. K. Chesterton wrote:

> The chief mark and element of insanity is reason used without root, reason in the void. The man who begins to think without the proper first principles goes mad, the man who begins to think at the wrong end.

At the same time, a faith that is accurate response to divine revelation grasps further truths which provide a fuller knowledge of the ends of human life and the appropriate means to encompass them. Human nature, so it turns out, is ordered to a superhuman goal. The supernatural is now the only way the good of our nature can actually be achieved. To cite Chesterton again:

> For Catholics it is a fundamental dogma of the Faith that all human beings, without any exception whatever, are specially made, were specially shaped and pointed like shining arrows, for the end of hitting the mark of Beatitude.

Mother Nature is always looking for the supernatural, whether she knows it or not.

So the first antidote to evil the Church offers is simply a true appreciation of the preciousness of goodness, and its intended efflorescence in the vision of God. (Notice how in this formulation, truth, goodness and beauty are conjoined not only with each other, but with movement toward God.) Unfortunately, there can be in the Church an excessive moral rigorism which puts people off. There can also be a laxity and indifference to the Church's own message that either sickens people or disappoints them but in either case drives them away. Both are avoided when her teaching is taken in its proper proportions and seen as satisfying, delighting and ultimately beatifying mind, will, emotions, all the person's powers. Freedom always needs educating. It is when it is educated that it is liberated, and it is properly taught when it is taught by truth.

Fighting vices by virtues

We can say at once that the ethics of Catholicism are far wider than we are used to in contemporary secular discourse in the West, just because those ethics revolve around the *virtues* – the entire range of dispositions which make for our moral flourishing. What since the Enlightenment we are more used to is the idea that central to morality are contracts made by rational consent on a basis of enlightened (precisely!) self-interest. From so bright a focus, many aspects of the good life which fail to fit that pattern slip all too easily into shadow. On the battlefield of the soul it is important to know where all – not just some – of the enemy battalions are situated.

That military metaphor governs perhaps the most influential evocation of the vices and virtues: the *Psychomachia* of the Latin Christian poet Prudentius, where these conflicting dispositions challenge each other like warriors before Troy in Homer. There is deadly conflict because while the main virtues are ways to be beautifully human, their opposites – the principal vices – are ways to be perfectly beastly.

For the ancient and mediaeval ethics that have become part and parcel of Catholicism's patrimony, the virtues are dispositions, habitual attitudes, which have the effect of making us harmonious, integrated personalities in tune with the rest of creation. They make us flourish precisely as human beings and in that way tend of their nature to make us happy. (That is true even if they cannot prevent unfortunate incidents happening to us – and if, on occasion, they may expose us to misfortune, as when, for example, someone with the virtue of courage keeps their place in a battle line during a just war, while the man who lacks that virtue runs away. In general, however, being courageous does help us to lead fuller lives.) The vices, by contrast, are dispositions, habitual attitudes, that have exactly the opposite effect to the virtues, shattering the harmony of the personality and destroying its integrity, as well as rupturing its unity with the rest of creation. Vices undermine people's flourishing as human beings and in that way tend to make them unhappy. (That is true even if vicious habits can sometimes bring accidental windfalls, as when someone who suffers from the vice of anger may be able to get his own way by displaying aggression more readily than other people do.)

The 'seven deadly sins' were picked out by ancient and mediaeval moralists as the worst of the vices, and that in two senses. First, they are the most destructive vices, the ones most likely to kill stone dead the humanity, and so the image of God, and thereby the grace of God, within us. Second, by a grisly kind of fruitfulness of their own, they originate other vicious patterns of behaviour beyond themselves. So the seven 'deadlies' are both the most destructive *and the most creative* of the vices. Thus, for instance, according to St Gregory the Great, the sin of avarice by which we love temporal things, especially riches, in inordinate fashion leads to hardness of heart towards the poor, anxiety about our own financial position, and dishonesty in commercial dealings with others. St Gregory manages to locate as many as seven 'daughters' of avarice' – treachery, fraud, deceit, perjury, restlessness, violence

134

and closing the heart to compassion. Already, on the basis of one deadly sin, that adds up to a fairly unattractive picture of a human being. The film *Seven* depicts, in the spirit of a mediaeval morality play, an unknown executioner picking off one after another individuals who embody representatively the deadly sins by arranging for their removal from the world in the manner best befitting their vice. But on leaving the cinema, we realise that our pleasure at seeing rough justice meted out to these characters rather than their possible reform is the result of the sin of pride by which we consider we have nothing in common with the morally ugly and so become indifferent to their fate.

That is a salutary discovery for the cinema-goer not least because once I develop a taste for one deadly sin I immediately become more prone to all the rest. Gluttony makes me lustful; avarice makes me envious of the goods and happiness of others; pride makes me slothful about my own growth in the virtues, and all of them generate anger, the last of the sin in this listing, when something or someone gets in the way of my perverse ambitions.

The tangled inter-connection of the vices makes it vital to realise the inter-locking unity of the virtues. While to name the virtues we must list them singly, they do not simply add up to a catalogue. They form a pattern, an ordered whole. Each is needed to perfect the rest, in a city of the self laid out with just streets and architectural proportions. A Catholic generosity of temper takes pleasure in multiplying the virtues, praising their range and variety. Tutored by the Gospel, it also treats *charity* as their 'form', the overarching structure where all find their place, and, whether they be natural virtues or supernatural, their proper role. By charity – along with faith and hope a 'theological' or God-conjoining virtue – we are able to love God more than all else, so that our lives are shaped by the love of God: our decisions so taken that they imply we prefer nothing else to him, and our actions such that they show we love him and will to share his love for others. In charity

we love God not simply as our maker but more charac-
teristically as our Freedom, who wishes to share with us
his life and happiness. Charity orientates the other virtues
towards their last end. All virtues whatsoever find their
value affirmed by their integration into the order of grace.
Yet the theological virtues are pre-eminent since (borrowing
a word from Aristotle) they have no 'mean': that is, it
never gets in the way of the good that we should have
more of them. We can never love God inordinately, just as
we can never believe in him excessively nor hope in him
too much.

Helps to the good life

Wise old Mother Church, with her bi-millenial experience,
has some tips up her sleeve, to diminish the reign of the
vices and extend the realm of the virtues.

'Good books'

Catholic literature purifies, heals and redeems the imagination. It is at its own level a vehicle of grace. *Shakespeare*'s
plays, for instance, correct the fallen tendency to presuppose
an anarchy in things which would be a denial of the divine
'fathering' of creation, for God is not a God of disorder:
they do this by insinuating a sense of cosmic order into our
vision of the world. Shakespeare's drama, moreover, is
pervaded by themes of repentance and redemption. The
poetry of *Hopkins* reveals a sacramental world that tells of
a Creator who in the Incarnation meets his own creature
face to face, and by his Passion redeems mortality. The
world is mounted in a drop of Christ's blood, and yet
preserves its own colours – Hopkins celebrates the utter
distinctiveness of things, each marked by 'instress' – the
pressure within a thing which maintains the coherence of
its 'inscape', its particular arrangement. An imagination
which had learned from Hopkins would not attempt

egoistically to gobble up the world. But it is not merely a matter of respecting things and persons. For Hopkins the Resurrection transforms the perpetual flux of a world where things come into being and pass out of it again into a triumphant pattern of redemption. *Tolkien's* epic *The Lord of the Rings* created an imaginative framework for the Christian experience of hope. The inhabitants of 'Middle Earth' come to believe in a moral dynamism in the universe to which each contributes freely but without knowing how it will all work. Evil is really malignant; it is not just imperfection. Mordor has no geographical limits; it is wherever its victims are. Tolkien emphasises the peculiar malice of possessiveness, especially in regard to persons. Violation of them produces, as with the 'ring-wraiths', exile from the healthful world, tormented exhaustion, failure of perception. (Revealingly, 'Mouth of Sauron', the lieutenant of the Tower of Barad-Dur, has forgotten his own name.) The fundamental superiority of good is symbolised by the light of Lorien, which pierces to the heart of darkness at Dol Goldur, but cannot itself be penetrated in return. Tolkien extols humility. The juxtaposition of the 'hobbits', lowly and unimpressive creatures, with grand adventures on the heroic scale, takes up the cry of the Virgin Mary in the *Magnificat,* 'He has lifted up the lowly' (Lk 1:52), and even Jesus' self-description, 'Learn from me; for I am gentle and humble in heart' (Mt 11:29). In *Chesterton,* wonder is what makes possible the imaginative concentration needed to discover the sacramental secret of the world, and thankfulness the appropriate response to it. In his novels and the short stories built around the priest-detective 'Father Brown', however, Chesterton moves gradually away from treating the imagination as the privileged mode of our exploration of the world to emphasising reason in defence of a Christian order against the irrationalities of modern life.

Holy fasts

Fasting and abstinence – literal counterparts of moral attitudes inculcated in the writers I have been discussing – are integral parts of the Church's penitential discipline. At a time when many people in the Western world have elected to be vegetarians, abstinence from flesh meats may seem to be no big deal – though for those who look forward to a succulent fillet steak, served *au poivre*, it retains its point. Fasting, however, is a different matter. Here both the amount and the elaborateness of food are seriously reduced. A good modern rule from America says: no snacks, no seconds, no desserts, no alcohol, though the canonical definition is simply one meal and one collation (or light refreshment). More heroic recipes are known. Fasting has different meanings in different religions, and is not always to be approved, any more than is all religion as such. Some fasting follows from an attempt to deify the self, to cross the boundary separating finite consciousness from infinite – a thing someone might well feel is happening if strange things befall the psyche owing to deprivation of food. This could be just silly, or devilishly perverse. The Christian saints – the Desert Fathers, for example – have often been prodigious fasters. But the meaning of their fasting was other. Christian fasting is an adjunct to holy warfare because it is an expression of hunger for God. Despite the sanctifying grace brought us by faith and the sacraments, and the indwelling of the Holy Trinity such grace makes possible, nevertheless, as the need for an 'antidote to evil' shows, we are in a sense not with God. He, Emmanuel, is with us. But we are not with him. We wander far off into what St Augustine calls the 'land of unlikeness'. But unless, between God and ourselves, there is co-presence, there is no full inter-relationship. We hunger materially in food that we may hunger spiritually for God. For really to want God is to intend all good. Such fasting is not simply a stratagem for reducing libidinal appetite which might only be relevant to the vice of lust. It tends to extirpate all vices by a re-direction of the personality as a whole.

A Christian Commonwealth

A very different kind of discipline but still in the category of restraint upon evil is provided by the Christian – the confessing, which is not to say, in some impossibly narrow or sectarian sense, the confessional – State. Liberalism – which from one point of view is legally contained anarchy – would hold that citizens as citizens, even in an overwhelmingly Catholic country, need not concern themselves with divine revelation, which affects only their private lives. On this view, all the Church should seek from civil society is freedom of action in the propagation of its own faith. It would be inappropriate for the State in any way to underwrite Christian beliefs and ethics as true and just. But the Second Vatican Council's *Declaration on Religious Freedom,* whilst insisting that, owing to the intrinsic dignity of the human person, even the erroneous conscience and its manifestations should be immune from civil interference (except where the common good or 'public order' is at stake), did not by any means intend to dismantle the idea of the Christian State. In the course of the century just ending, the Liberal State – that State which defines itself by its equidistance from all religions and wider value systems – has maintained itself only with difficulty against such forces as Marxism-Leninism, Fascism and Islamic fundamentalism. Who knows what Godless or anti-humane ideologies may not surface in the future? Liberalism has no antidote to evil: its only mantra – so uninformative as to be useless to most people – is, Be responsible in making choices. With all necessary safeguards for the conscientious rights of minorities, should not the members of a largely Christian society, when acting as a civil community, seek to recognise and realise the will of God, both natural and revealed, putting in place social practice that helps to embody that will, just as they do as private individuals? Nations born or re-born in the baptismal covenant need to recover their spiritual roots in Christian civilisation, States indebted to that civilisation to admit the public relevance of Christian tradition in their law-making. The wisdom of the Church's social teaching can help them avoid both the atomised individualism and the excessive collectivism which have so damaged the social organism in modern times. Public life needs right order, and the ethos of a 'civilisation of love'. The aim is not to make civil society, and the State which presides in it, a surrogate for the Church but in the words of an Anglican expositor of T. S. Eliot's social criticism, 'to make the sanctification of souls a little less difficult'. One ecumenical agreement it should be easy to reach is saying Amen to that.

Intercession

Jesus remarks of the demons, 'This kind can come out only through *prayer and* fasting' (Mark 9:29, italics [obviously!] added). Whether for ourselves or others we can ask to be delivered from evil: that is the culminating petition of the *Pater*, the 'Lord's Prayer'. Catholics seek in this context the intercession of the saints, as well as those who are living a consecrated life as monks and nuns. The Byzantine icon known as the Deesis, the 'Intercession' where the Mother of God, and the Holy Forerunner, John the Baptist, stand on either side of the seated Christ and incline towards him, often holding scrolls carrying the petitioners' prayers, beautifully exemplifies the first theme. It is foolishness not to invoke the aid of humanity's most powerful advocates before God. The faithful Christian presents his request, but the saints pass it on to Christ, adding entreaty of their own. Monasticism must also be mentioned here. Those who are living a life of perfect surrender to God (of course monasteries vary in their fervour, as do their members) are mighty intercessors for

Christendom and those harassed by evil within it. We do not know how much we owe to them, how many more horrors, personal and corporate, they enable us to avoid. Against the spiritual hosts of wickedness, they are the defenders of the walls.

Homecoming

*'... the resurrection of the body and
life everlasting...'*

Yield to his Siege, wise Soul, and see
Your Triumph in his Victory.
Disband dull Feares, give Faith the day:
To save your Life, kill your Delay.
'Tis Cowardise that keeps this field;
And want of Courage not to Yield.
Yield then, O yield, that Love may win
The Fort at last, and let Life in.
Yield quickly, lest perhaps you prove
Death's Prey, before the Prize of Love.
This Fort of your Fair Self if't be not wone,
He is repuls'd indeed, but You're undone.

Death

THE Church has never reconciled herself to the fact of
human death as we know it. Death is the internal destruction
of the body–soul unity of man. It is also the external
destruction of friendship and relationship. Like St Paul,
Catholicism sees death (again, *as we know it*) as the result
of a terrible breakdown in God's plan. 'Sin came into the
world through one man, and death came through sin' (Rom
5:12). In this, the disciples of Jesus are like their Master
who wept at the grave of Lazarus his friend, and cried into
the darkness of the tomb, 'Lazarus, come out!' (Jn 11:43).
The younger we are the less we tend to have any experience
of bereavement, while the old, by contrast, often feel
themselves to be simply survivors of the dead. But the less

experience we have, the more important it is to maintain a sense of the very great seriousness of dying. A grizzled old lady to whom I once took Holy Communion in a town in the central industrial belt of Scotland said, 'The Catholic religion is a hard one to live in, but an easy one to die in'. We have to beware of turning that formula upside down, and leaving people unprepared for their own dying, without a scenario, or a spiritual geography for the realm of death such as the Catholic doctrine of Purgatory provides. Contemporary sensibility, which lacks such a map, can lead the Church's members to cope with death by sentimentalisation: to canonise all the departed faithful and unfaithful and every gradation in between; to turn the Requiem Mass from a sacrifice of expiation into a remembrance service.

That needs to be resisted not just in the name of orthodoxy but of simple human reality. The single most important *personal* function religion plays in people's lives is to enable them to face their own deaths and those of others, to grieve and turn the energy of grief to good use in a spiritual self-offering that will help the dead to be purified for the vision of God. That is what Catholics are doing when they celebrate the Requiem Mass, or have Masses said for what Italians call *i suoi cari defunti*, 'their dear departed'. It is because Jesus Christ is so completely the only Mediator between God and man that he can freely make us in our turn into mediators of him – can take our prayers and sacrifices into his own self-offering to the Father and so make them fruitful for life everlasting.

Destiny in God

To speak of temporal creatures such as ourselves coming home to eternity sounds at first hearing like a contradiction in terms. But eternity is not timeless in an abstract, negative sense, in the way a number – 0 or 666 – could be said to be. Eternity embraces all time, all duration, just as the infinite explains all instances of the finite. What the mystery of the Ascension told us in chapter 5 is that we are not to be swallowed up by the Eternal but to be cherished in our particularity by it – though this will be a particularity liberated from everything petty, constraining, egotistic.

Catholics speak of the 'Four Last Things': Death, Judgement, Heaven and Hell, with Purgatory squeezed somewhere in between Judgement and Heaven in that list. But really there is only one 'Last Thing' and it is not a thing at all but the Archetype of all personhood, God himself – the triune God, naturally, made accessible to us in the humanity of our Lord. Balthasar wrote:

> God is the 'last thing' of the creature. Gained, he is Heaven; lost, he is Hell; examining, he is judgement; purifying, he is Purgatory. To him finite being dies, and through, to and in him it rises. But this is God as he presents himself to the world, that is, in his Son, Jesus Christ, who is the revelation of God and therefore the whole essence of the last things.

Heaven is the vision of God in a social setting. Its centre is the 'icon' that is the risen humanity of Christ, in whom we see the everlasting exchange of love that flows from the Father, the Fount. But in heaven they also experience the work and grace of God in the holy people whom the Blood of Jesus Christ has won through the triumphs of grace in the saints. As in that masterpiece of fourteenth-century English courtly art the *Wilton Diptych*, the blessed look not only at the earthbound in expectation but also at each other in friendship. Among the saints whose sight will ravish us, the Mother of God holds the highest place. As Beatrice asks Dante in the *Paradiso*:

> Why does my face so enamour thee that thou dost not turn to the fair garden that flowers under the rays of Christ? There is the Rose in which the divine Word was made flesh.

144

It should be apparent that, as the goal of creation and redemption, the whole purpose of the divine plan for the world, it is Heaven that fills the eschatological imagination of Catholics. Hell is the real possibility of Heaven's loss. It has no meaning in and of itself, for it is the destruction (for me if I suffer it, for the damned) of meaning's comprehensive context and ultimate ground. It is a terrible warning to malice, and, in that sense, salutary. Purgatory – the 'intermediate state' – has, by definition, nothing final about it. We may, however, hazard a guess that it is where most people now are. Most of us die without fully appreciating the rich stream of graces this book has described, without, too, making our due contribution to the repair of a damaged world. In Purgatory that appropriation in depth, that healing reparation, can happen, in the peaceful yet happy suffering that is therapeutic delay in proceeding to the vision of the Father's face.

Can there be more even than this to coming home? Yes, for there remains the extension to bodies of the bliss of grace in souls. At that final consummation of cosmic purpose in the Parousia of the Lord, we shall take things in, no doubt, at our own pace. That is only consistent with Incarnation. In a manner appropriate to our humanity, we shall be conscious of the transfiguration of the wider cosmos, indeed thrill to it, know it in our fingertips. Without attempting to enter here upon the question, Will there be asphodels, or phlox drummondii for that matter, in the new creation?, or, Will Leo the lilac-point Birman make it there?, we can at least say, everything abidingly valuable in the old creation will be preserved, while the Word through whom all things were made will surprise us anew. St Bede wrote in his commentary on the Apocalypse:

> Christ is the morning star who when the night of this world is past promises and reveals to his saints the light of life and of everlasting day.

That light must fall on something, that day dawn on some

scene, and surely it will be on that renewed world. And this will be the Father's final gift of love.

My hope for this small book is that it may contribute in a modest way to a reflorescence of English Catholicism in the twenty-first century comparable to that Victorian Catholic revival which was so marked a feature of the nineteenth, and whose hard-won gains recent decades have often squandered. So I may as well end my substantive text with a hymn-fragment from one of that revival's writers which strikes the right note of eschatological generosity, the hope that springs eternal from the heart of the Church.

> There is plentiful redemption
> In the blood that has been shed;
> There is joy for all the members
> In the sorrows of the Head.
>
> There is grace enough for thousands
> Of new worlds as great as this;
> There is room for fresh creations
> In that upper home of bliss.

Conclusion

'... Amen.'

Lady and Queen and Mystery manifold
And very Regent of th'untroubled sky,
Whom in a dream St Hilda did behold
And heard a woodland music passing by:
You shall receive me when the clouds are high
With evening and the sheep attain the fold.
This is the faith that I have held and hold,
And this is that in which I mean to die.

Steep are the seas and savaging and cold
In broken waters terrible to try;
And vast against the winter night the wold,
And harbourless for any sail to lie.
But you shall lead me to the lights, and I
Shall hymn you in a harbour story told.
This is the faith that I have held and hold,
And this is that in which I mean to die.

Help of the half-defeated, House of gold,
Shrine of the Sword, and Tower of Ivory;
Splendour apart, supreme and aureoled,
The Battler's vision and the World's reply.
You shall restore me, O my last Ally,
To vengence and the glories of the bold.
This is the faith that I have held and hold,
And this is that in which I mean to die.

Envoi
Prince of the degradations, bought and sold,
These verses, written in your crumbling sty,

Proclaim the faith that I have held and hold
And publish that in which I mean to die.

MY invitation to the reader to 'come to the Father' by coming to share the faith of the Catholic Church is itself coming to an end. Before drawing the threads together, one important caveat must be mentioned. Cardinal Newman once defined his purpose as to make the Church fit for converts to live in. Certainly there is much to be done to enable the treasures of Catholic faith and ethos to become more apparent for what they really are. In my book *Christendom Awake* I mention a number of things to be desired and, since they are so vital to evangelisation, I may be allowed to repeat them here. They include:

– a renaissance of doctrine in catechesis and preaching: necessary if we are to show that, as *Come to the Father* has tried to exemplify, revelation is the greatest truth ever known

– a re-enchanting of the liturgy so that by language, gesture, image, music, it brings us before the beauty of the Kingdom

– a recovery of metaphysics, so as to demonstrate how the bits and pieces of ideas now in common currency can be exchanged for a coherent philosophy of the created order

– a renewed Christian political thinking which is not just about favouring the poor, but must deal with the wider question of combining order and spontaneity within a spacious civil life under God (presumably one does not 'opt for the poor' so that they can have 1.5 television sets on which to watch soap operas!)

– the revivification of the family through uniting, wherever possible, the domestic and the productive, home and work

148

- the resacralising of art and architecture so that they can again bring us echoes of the divine order as well as of the meanings men make within it

- recovering a truly Catholic reading of the Scriptures, and above all of the Gospels, on the understanding that we shall find there what liturgy and doctrine tell us of, the divine-human Christ who accepted the union of the two natures in himself for our salvation. (What a state Islam would be in if Muslim scholars held as many contradictory views of what Mohammed was up to as exegetes often do nowadays about the aims of Jesus!)

- rediscovering the imaginative ways in which our poets have commended the moral truths defended by the Church (for instance, abortion) in a fashion that can revivify people's dulled sensibilities in a culture that has grown comfortable with ethical errors in whole regions of life. It is important to recall that defeatism can be thwarted by the processes of imagination.

The faith of the Catholic Church furnishes a whole host of cues for improving the performance of the empirical Catholic Church – clergy and laity – in this or that place.

It is often thought that Catholics are anti-intellectual, since their religion relies on faith. In this study I have suggested some of the rational underpinnings of Catholicism – the rational preamble to revealed faith. I have concentrated more, however, on the way reason fructifies under the sun of revelation, so that its fullest and most competent exercise, where metaphysics and morals are concerned, is only possible through faith, through grace, through Christ. Catholics indeed, as the Scholastic tradition shows, have enormous respect for reason, and if their way of expressing that respect differs from those common among their unbelieving contemporaries, that is because for them truth always receives its 'finality', its goal, from love. We make precisions so as to love more, to see more of the great things the love of God has done in creating, redeeming, and transfiguring the world through Jesus Christ and his Spirit and to respond to that love the more eagerly ourselves.

And so I make no apology that in this book I have not dwelt on the difficulties which theologians of a more quizzical temper deal in. Doubtless such figures have their uses as grit in oysters. But one cannot always be thinking in the critical or interrogatory mode. Mental fatigue inevitably overcomes one who tries. The mind was meant to know truth, to consume it and feed off it, not just to press its nose against an intellectual shop-window. Without constructive and affirmatory thinking, the theological intellect grows spectre-thin and dies. This short study has been an exercise in imaginative orthodoxy. It was written not for theological critics, dissenting or otherwise, but for people who are crying out for spiritual bread and would not thank me for the gift of a stone.

Here at any rate is a faith one can live by as countless souls in a huge variety of times and places have discovered. Here is a context in which one can breathe after attempting survival in that post-modern world where in the last resort everything is confined, cramped and pinched by that most narrowing of all imperatives, 'Construct identity, and reality, for yourself!' Good reader, pass over the market opportunity to make yourself up, and allow grace to do it for you in the way the redemptive Creator, more intimate to you than you are to yourself, knows how. This is the wider room into which the saints and mystics of the Church invite you, where not even the sky is the limit.

An altar-piece, now lost, once in Rome, showed Richard II, the last Plantagenet of the direct line, offering to the Virgin a 'globe' or 'pattern' of England which may be echoed in the somewhat inscrutable tiny orb atop the flag of the Resurrection in the *Wilton Diptych*. (It appears, at any rate, to show a portion of earth between sea and sky.) The painted altar-piece bore the inscription, 'This is your dowry, O holy Virgin. Therefore rule over it, O Mary'. In the *Diptych*, the king receives back from Christ the realm he had given in homage to the Mother of the Lord. In so doing he rules it not by right of blood line chiefly but by transcendent authorisation. No kingdom that has known the Gospel can forget its claims. I have tried to show in this book why they are worth asserting.

'All with Peter to Jesus through Mary!' has been taken – and well taken – as a summary of the Catholic faith and its hope for the world. But the Spirit thus brings us to Jesus so that we may *come to the Father*. For anyone who thinks the contents of the Creed remotely credible, not to consider conversion risks incurring the opprobrium that justly attaches to ingratitude. In the words of a novelist yet to come (so far as I know) to such faith:

> It is the prodigal who does not return who makes the idea of goodness a mockery.

Sources for citations

Introduction

'O God of earth and altar…' G. K. Chesterton, 'A Hymn', in *The Collected Poems of G. K. Chesterton* (London: Methuen and Co., 1937, 6th edition), pp. 146-147.

'The water crept…' E. M. Forster, *Howard's End* (Harmondsworth: Penguin Books, 1983), p. 178.

Chapter 1, Faith in Truth

'Firmly I believe…' John Henry Newman, 'The Dream of Gerontius' in *Newman. Prose and Poetry*, selected by Geoffrey Tillotson (London: Rupert Hart Davis, 1957), pp. 814-815.

'O Light invisible…' T. S. Eliot, 'Choruses from "The Rock", X', in *Collected Poems, 1909-1962*, by T. S. Eliot (London: Faber and Faber, 1963; 1974), pp. 183-184.

Chapter 2, Fathering the Creation

'Glory be to God…' Gerard Manley Hopkins, 'Pied Beauty', in *The Poems of Gerard Manley Hopkins*, edited by W. H. Gardner and N. H. Mackenzie (London: Oxford University Press, 1970), pp. 69-70.

'[It] deals out…' Gerard Manley Hopkins, 'As kingfishers catch fire', ibid., p. 90.

'Man is the perfection… ' St Francis of Sales, *Traité de l'Amour de Dieu,* X. 1.

'Adam was created…' Cyril of Alexandria, *Commentary on the Epistle to the Romans*, V. 18.

Chapter 3, The Fleshtaking

'The poet's imageries…' Alice Meynell, 'The Courts: a Figure of the Epiphany', in *The Poems of Alice Meynell.*

Complete Edition (London: Burns, Oates and Washbourne, 1923), p. 87.

'an amnesiac Christmas…' André Frossard, *Dieu existe. Je l'ai rencontré* Paris: Fayard, 1969), p. 29.

Chapter 4, The Rose in the Crown

'There is no rose…' Anonymous, 'Rosa mystica', in *A Mediaeval Anthology. Being Lyrics and Other Short Poems Chiefly Religious*, collected and modernised by Mary G. Segar (London: Longmans, Green and Co., 1915), p. 65.

'… as you pass' Hilaire Belloc, 'Sonnet VII', in *Sonnets and Verse* (London: Duckworth 1923; 1938), p. 9.

'It all hangs…' David Jones, 'Mabinog's Liturgy', in *The Anathemata. Fragments of an Attempted Writing* (London: Faber and Faber, 1952; 1972), p. 214.

'It was His ordinance… ' Frederick William Faber, *The Foot of the Cross* (London: Derby (printed), 1858), pp. 33, 378-379.

'Christ alone is the perfect Mediator…' Thomas Aquinas, *Summa Theologiae*, IIIa., q. 26, a.1.

Chapter 5, Ultimate Sacrifice

'Rise, heir of fresh eternity…' Richard Crashaw, 'Easter Day', in *Silver Poets of the Seventeenth Century*, edited by G. A. E. Parfitt (London: Dent, and Totowa, N.J.: Rowman and Littlefield, 1974), p. 154.

'The royal door…' Cardinal Roger Etchegaray, 'Foreword', *God, the Father of Mercy*. Prepared by the Theological–Historical Commission for the Great Jubilee of the Year 2000 (New York: Crossroad, 1998), p.9.

'Since it was so…' *The Cloud of Unknowing. And other Treatises by an English Mystic of the Fourteenth Century*. With a Commentary on *The Cloud* by Fr Augustine Baker, O.S.B. Edited by Dom Justin McCann, Monk of Ampleforth (London: Burns Oates and Washbourne, 1924), pp. 144-145.

Chapter 6, Gracious Spirit

'Creator Spirit…' John Dryden, 'Veni Creator Spiritus, Translated in Paraphrase', in *The Poems and Fables of John Dryden*, edited by James Kinsley (Oxford: Oxford University Press, 1958; 1962; 1970), pp. 486-487.

Chapter 7, Our Mother the Church

'Who is She…' Francis Thompson, 'Assumpta Maria', in *The Oxford Book of English Mystical Verse*, chosen by D. H. S. Nicholson and A. H. E. Lee (Oxford: Clarendon Press, 1917; 1932), p. 422.

Chapter 8, Holy Persons, Holy Gifts

'His hands conjoined…' David Jones, 'The Kensington Mass' in *The Roman Quarry, and Other Sequences,* edited by Harman Grisewood and Rene Hague (London: Agenda Editions, 1981), p. 88.

'The rosary is said…' Patrick Kavanagh, *Lough Derg* (The Curragh: Goldsmith Press, 1978), p. 11.

'Thus we, at last,…' *The Martyrdom of Polycarp*, XVIII.

'Now that God…' John of Damascus, *On the Holy Images*, I. 16.

Chapter 9, Antidote to Evil

'Shall I confess…' William Alabaster, 'Sonnet 52', in *The Sonnets*, edited by G. M. Story and Helen Gardner (Oxford: Oxford University Press, 1959).

'It is often argued… ' David Selbourne, *Moral Evasion* (London: Centre for Policy Studies, 1998), pp. 3-5.

'The chief mark and element…' G. K. Chesterton, *Orthodoxy* (1908; repr. London: Hodder and Stoughton, 1996), p. 30.

'For Catholics…' G. K. Chesterton, *The Thing* (London: Sheed and Ward, 1929), p. 26.

'To make the sanctification...' David Edwards, 'Introduction', in T. S. Eliot, *The Idea of a Christian Society, and Other Writings* (London: Faber and Faber, 1939; 1982), p. 31.

Chapter 10, Homecoming

'Yield to his Siege...' Richard Crashaw, 'A Letter to the Countess of Denbigh against Irresolution and Delay in Matters of Religion', in *The Metaphysical Poets*, introduced and edited by Helen Gardner (Harmondsworth: Penguin, 1972), p. 217.

'God is the "last thing" of the creature...' Hans Urs von Balthasar, *Sponsa Verbi. Skizzen zur Theologie, II* (Einsiedeln: Johannes Verlag, 1961), p. 282.

'Why does my face...' Dante, *Paradiso*, canto XXIII, in *The Divine Comedy of Dante Alighieri*. Italian text with translation and comment by John D. Sinclair (London: Oxford University Press, 1971), p. 335.

'Christ is the morning star...' Bede the Venerable, *Commentary on the Apocalypse*, 2:28.

'There is plentiful redemption...' F. W. Faber, 'There's a wideness in God's mercy', text reprinted in *The New English Hymnal* (Norwich: The Canterbury Press, 1986), p. 668.

Conclusion

'Lady and Queen...' Hilaire Belloc, 'Ballade to our Lady of Czestochowa', in *Sonnets and Verse*, op. cit., pp. 150-151.

'It is the prodigal...' Anita Brookner, *Family and Friends* (London: Triad Grafton, 1985; 1993), p.167.

The Mystical Language of Icons
Solrunn Ness

In this beautifully colour-illustrated volume, the author –
one of Europe's most highly regarded icon painters –
explains in detail many of the most well recognised icon
paintings. The book offers a thorough historical and
theological background to the tradition of Orthodox iconography. Size: 210mm x 300mm.

ISBN 085439 584 9 96pp h/b £15.99

Spiritual Direction
Janet K. Ruffing

A book for both novice and experienced Spiritual directors.
It explores the dynamics of lifelong Spiritual development,
desire and resistance, the Spiritual Exercises in light of
women's experience, the significance of operative theology
in one's spiritual story, the significance of gender identity
in prayer and transference and counter-transference in
directee and director.

ISBN 085439 609 8 184pp £9.99

Sex: What the Catholic Church Teaches
John Redford

In a clear Question-and-Answer format the author draws
on the Bible and the Catechism of the Catholic Church, as
well as on his own experience as a pastor, to show how
positive Catholic doctrine on sex really is. An invaluable
book for schools, marriage preparation classes, candidates
undergoing RCIA or anyone who wants to know what the
Catholic Church teaches on this important subject and why.

ISBN 085439 599 7 208pp £6.99

Our Father
James Harkess

A new Catholic's daily conversation with God. An in-depth analysis of the seven petitions of the Lord's Prayer. Each chapter is followed by extended prayers, together with a commentary on those prayers.

ISBN 085439 529 6   176pp   £7.99

The Eucharist Yesterday and Today
Basil Pennington

Now in its second edition this book draws from the author's years in the priesthood and vast knowledge of the liturgy in other times and places. He evokes the deepest meanings of the Eucharistic celebration. The Roman liturgy, the Byzantine liturgy and even some contemporary celebrations come alive.

ISBN 085439 241 6   176pp   £7.99

A Light for Your Path
Anton Sammut

Using a varied and balanced collection of subjects, each illustrated with a story and further explained with a thought, a prayer or a quote, this book will be a source of encouragement in times of difficulty. It will inspire you to reach out to others with greater love and compassion and to be more patient and understanding; it will comfort you and help you to maintain your own inner peace and tranquillity when you are under stress; and it will keep you serene and humble in times of triumph and success. Written to give encouragement to young people, adult readers of any age and of any religious belief or denomination will find this book a unique source of inspiration, lighting the pathway on the journey of life.

ISBN 085439 614 4   216pp   £7.95

Knowing Jesus in the World
Praying with Teilhard de Chardin
Robert Faricy & Lucy Rooney

Gradually, Teilhard de Chardin's ideas have come to be appreciated. In 1981 Cardinal Casaroli praised Teilhard at the UNESCO celebration of the centenary of Teilhard's birth. Jesuit Father General Peter-Hans Kolvenbach, in 1995 wrote in praise of Teilhard to the International Teilhard de Chardin Conference, on the fortieth anniversary of Teilhard's death. Fr Kolvenbach has also written the preface to this book.

ISBN 085439 575 X   128pp   £4.99

A Short Introduction to the Catholic Church
Severino Dianich

This book deals with what people think of the Church, how it really is from the inside, what is needed in the Church, the difficult relationship between the Church and the world, the past and the future.

ISBN 085439 490 7   110pp   £5.50

A Short Introduction to the Apostles' Creed
Bruno Forte

The author, one of the leading theologians of our day, reflects on the faith of Christians in a simple and enlightened way. This brief introduction presents a concise theological and spiritual commentary on the essentials of the Catholic faith.

ISBN 085439 464 8   128pp   £4.95